Contents

Betania Cardigan 2

Effortless Cardigan 8

Comfy Stripe Cardigan 12

Birger Cardigan 16

Clusterwell Cardigan 20

Emelio Cardigan 25

Drapey Cardigan 30

Back to Basics Knit Cardigan 34

Freya Cardigan 38

Light 'N Easy Cardigan..................................... 42

Lille Cardigan... 46

Reading Room Cardigan................................. 50

Vogar Cardigan 54

Top Down Raglan Cardigan 60

High Plains Cardigan 64

Betania Cardigan

Intermediate

SIZES
X/S (M/L, 1X/2X).

MEASUREMENTS
Finished Bust 40 (49, 58)"/101.5 (124.5, 147.5)cm
Finished Length 32 (34, 36)"/81.5 (86.5, 91.5)cm

MATERIALS
YARN
LION BRAND® Wool-Ease® Thick & Quick®, 6oz/170g balls, each approx 106yd/97m (acrylic/wool)
- 5 (6, 7) balls in #149 Charcoal (A)
- 4 (5, 6) balls in #612 Coney Island (B)
- 2 (3, 3) balls in #609 Moonlight (C)
- 3 (3, 4) balls in #535 River Run (D)
- 1 (2, 2) balls in #154 Grey Marble (E)

NEEDLES
- One size 13 (9mm) circular knitting needle, 32"/81.5cm long, *or size to obtain gauge*
- One size 11 (8mm) circular knitting needle, 40"/101.5cm long

NOTIONS
- Stitch markers
- Stitch holders
- Tapestry needle

GAUGE
9 sts + 12 rows = approx 4"/10cm in St st using larger needle.
BE SURE TO CHECK YOUR GAUGE.

K1, P1 RIB
(over an odd number of sts)
Row 1 K1, *p1, k1; rep from * to end.
Row 2 K the knit sts and p the purl sts.
Rep Row 2 for K1, P1 Rib.

NOTES
1) Cardigan is worked in 5 pieces: Back, Left Front, Right Front, and 2 Sleeves.
2) Yarn colors are changed to make stripes.
3) Stitches for the front bands and collar are picked up along front edge Cardigan.
4) Front bands and collar are shaped by working short rows. Short rows are rows that are worked over a portion of the stitchess in a row, leaving the remaining stitches unworked. To work short rows, the pattern instructions will tell you to "turn" before you reach the end of row.
5) A circular needle is used to accommodate the number of stitches. Work back and forth with the circular needle as if working on straight needles.

STRIPE SEQUENCE
*Work 12 rows with A, 14 rows with B, 8 rows with C, 10 rows with D, 6 rows with E; rep from * for Stripe Sequence.

CARDIGAN
BACK
With smaller needle and A, cast on 55 (65, 75) sts.
Row 1 (RS) With A, work Row 1 of K1, P1 Rib.
Rows 2–12 Continue in K1, P1 Rib changing color following Stripe Sequence.

Body
Change to larger needle.
Changing color following Stripe Sequence, work in St st (k on RS, p on WS) until piece measures approx 4"/10cm above rib, end with a WS row as last row you work.
***Dec Row (RS)** K1, k2tog, k to last 3 sts, ssk, k1—53 (63, 73) sts.

Betania Cardigan

Continue in St st, changing color following Stripe Sequence, for 4"/10cm, end with a WS row as last row you work.

Rep from * 3 more times—47 (57, 67) sts.

Rep Dec Row—45 (55, 65) sts.

Continue in St st, changing color following Stripe Sequence, until piece measures approx 32 (34, 36)"/81.5 (86.5, 91.5)cm from beg.

Bind off.

POCKET LININGS

With larger needle and D, cast on 17 sts.

Work in St st until piece measures approx 9 (10, 11)"/23 (25.5, 28)cm from beg, end with a WS row as last row you work. Place these sts on a holder.

Rep for 2nd pocket lining.

LEFT FRONT

With smaller needle and A, cast on 25 (29, 33) sts.

Row 1 (RS) With A, work Row 1 of K1, P1 Rib.

Rows 2–12 Continue in K1, P1 Rib changing color following Stripe Sequence.

Body

Change to larger needle.

Continue to change color following Stripe Sequence.

Row 1 (RS) K5 (7, 9), pm, work K1, P1 Rib as established over next 17 sts, pm, k3 (5, 7).

Row 2 P to marker, sm, work K1, P1 Rib to next marker, sm, p to end.

Row 3 K to marker, sm, work K1, P1 Rib to next marker, sm, k to end.

Row 4 P to marker, sm, work K1, P1 Rib to next marker, sm, p to end.

Rows 5–14 Rep last 2 rows 5 more times.

Dec Row 15 K1, k2tog, k to marker, sm, work K1, P1 Rib to next marker, sm, k to end—24 (28, 32) sts.

Rows 16–29 Rep Rows 2–15—23 (27, 31) sts.

Rows 30–31 (30–33, 30–35) Rep Rows 2 and 3 for 1 (2, 3) times.

Join pocket lining

Remove markers while working next row.

Row 32 (34, 36) P to marker, bind off 17 sts between markers, p to end.

Row 33 (35, 37) K to bound-off sts; from RS, k across sts of one Pocket Lining from holder, k to end.

Next 9 (7, 5) rows Work in St st.

Dec row 43 K1, k2tog, k to end—22 (26, 30) sts.

Rows 44–48 (44–54, 44–56) Work in St st for 5 (11, 13) rows.

Size XS/S ONLY—Shape neck

Row 49 K to last 3 sts, ssk, k1—21 sts.

Work in St st for 7 rows.

Row 57 Rep Row 43—20 sts.

Row 58 Purl.
Row 59 Rep Row 49—19 sts.
Work in St st for 9 rows.
Row 69 Rep Row 49—18 sts.
Row 70 Purl.
Row 71 Rep Row 43—17 sts.

Size M/L ONLY—Shape neck
Row 55 K to last 3 sts, ssk, k1—25 sts.
Row 56 Purl.
Row 57 Rep Row 43—24 sts.
Work in St st for 7 rows.
Row 65 Rep Row 55—23 sts.
Work in St st for 5 rows.
Row 71 Rep Row 43—22 sts.

Size 1X/2X ONLY—Shape neck
Row 57 Rep Row 43—29 sts.
Work in St st for 3 rows.
Row 61 (RS) K to last 3 sts, ssk, k1—28 sts.
Work in St st for 9 rows.
Row 71 K1, k2tog, k to last 3 sts, ssk, k1—26 sts.

All sizes
Work in St st for 7 (3, 9) rows.
Row 79 (75, 81) K to last 3 sts, ssk, k1—16 (21, 25) sts.
Work in St st for 9 rows.
Row 89 (85, 91) K to last 3 sts, ssk, k1—15 (20, 24) sts.
Rep last 10 rows 0 (1, 1) more time(s)—15 (19, 23) sts.
Work even in St st until piece measures same as Back.
Bind off.

RIGHT FRONT
With smaller needle and A, cast on 25 (29, 33) sts.
Row 1 (RS) With A, work Row 1 of K1, P1 Rib.
Rows 2–12 Continue in K1, P1 Rib changing color following Stripe Sequence.

Body
Change to larger needle.
Continue to change color following Stripe Sequence.
Row 1 (RS) K3 (5, 7), pm, work K1, P1 Rib as established over next 17 sts, pm, k5 (7, 9).
Row 2 P to marker, sm, work K1, P1 Rib to next marker, sm, p to end.
Row 3 K to marker, sm, work K1, P1 Rib to next marker, sm, k to end.
Row 4 P to marker, sm, work K1, P1 Rib to next marker, sm, p to end.
Rows 5–14 Rep last 2 rows 5 more times.
Dec Row 15 K to marker, sm, work K1, p1 Rib to next marker, sm, k to last 3 sts, ssk, k1—24 (28, 32) sts.
Rows 16–29 Rep Rows 2–15—23 (27, 31) sts.
Rows 30–31 (30–33, 30–35) Rep Rows 2 and 3 for 1 (2, 3) times.

Join pocket lining
Remove markers while working next row.
Row 32 (34, 36) P to marker, bind off 17 sts between markers, p to end.
Row 33 (35, 37) K to bound-off sts; from RS, k across sts of 2nd Pocket Lining from holder, k to end.
Rows 34–42 (36–42, 38–42) Work in St st for 9 (7, 5) rows.
Dec Row 43 K to last 3 sts, ssk, k1—22 (26, 30) sts.
Rows 44–48 (44–54, 44–56) Work in St st for 5 (11, 13) rows.

Size XS/S ONLY—Shape neck
Row 49 K1, k2tog, k to end—21 sts.
Work in St st for 7 rows.
Row 57 Rep Row 43—20 sts.
Row 58 Purl.
Row 59 Rep Row 49—19 sts.
Work in St st for 9 rows.
Row 69 Rep Row 49—18 sts.
Row 70 Purl.
Row 71 Rep Row 43—17 sts.

Size M/L ONLY—Shape neck
Row 55 K1, k2tog, k to end—25 sts.
Row 56 Purl.
Row 57 Rep Row 43—24 sts.
Work in St st for 7 rows.
Row 65 Rep Row 55—23 sts.
Work in St st for 5 rows.
Row 71 Rep Row 43—22 sts.

Betania Cardigan

Size 1X/2X ONLY—Shape neck
Row 57 Rep Row 43—29 sts.
Work in St st for 3 rows.
Row 61 (RS) K1, k2tog, k to end—28 sts.
Work in St st for 9 rows.
Row 71 K1, k2tog, k to last 3 sts, ssk, k1—26 sts.

All sizes
Work in St st for 7 (3, 9) rows.
Row 79 (75, 81) K1, k2tog, k to end—16 (21, 25) sts.
Work in St st for 9 rows.
Row 89 (85, 91) K1, k2tog, k to end—15 (20, 24) sts.
Rep last 10 rows 0 (1, 1) more time(s)—15 (19, 23) sts.
Work even in St st until piece measures same as Back. Bind off.

SLEEVES
With smaller needle and A, cast on 25 (27, 29) sts.
Work rib as for Back.
Change to larger needle.
Continuing to change color following Stripe Sequence, and beg with a WS (purl) row, work in St st for 3 rows.
Inc Row K1, M1, k to last st, M1, k1—27 (29, 31) sts.
Rep last 4 rows 11 (12, 13) more times—49 (53, 57) sts.
Work even in St st until piece measures about 23"/58.5cm from beg. Bind off.

FINISHING
Sew shoulder seams.

Front bands and collar
Note Do not wrap stitches before turning work for a short row—this design works beautifully without the wraps.
Row 1 (RS) From RS with smaller needle and A, beg at lower Right Front corner, pick up and k 1 st in end of each row along Right Front edge to beg of neck shaping, pm, pick up and k 1 st in end of each row to right shoulder, pick up and k 1 st in each st across back neck, pick up and k 1 st in end of each row from left shoulder to beg of neck shaping, pm, pick up and k 1 st in end of each row along Left Front edge to lower Left Front corner. Pick up an additional st if needed to ensure that you have an odd number of sts.
Work back and forth in rows on circular needle as if working with straight needles. Slip markers as you come to them.

Row 2 Work Row 1 of K1, P1 Rib.

Row 3 Work K1, P1 Rib.

Row 4 Work K1, P1 Rib to 10 sts before 2nd marker (on Right Front), TURN.

Row 5 Work K1, P1 Rib to 10 sts before next marker (on Left Front), TURN.

Row 6 Work K1, P1 Rib to end.

Row 7 Work K1, P1 Rib.

Row 8 Work K1, P1 Rib to 8 sts before 2nd marker (on Right Front), TURN.

Row 9 Work K1, P1 Rib to 8 sts before next marker (on Left Front), TURN.

Row 10 Work K1, P1 Rib to end.

Row 11 Work K1, P1 Rib.

Row 12 Work K1, P1 Rib to 6 sts before 2nd marker (on Right Front), TURN.

Row 13 Work K1, P1 Rib to 6 sts before next marker (on Left Front), TURN.

Row 14 Work K1, P1 Rib to end.

Row 15 Work K1, P1 Rib.

Row 16 Work K1, P1 Rib to 4 sts before 2nd marker (on Right Front), TURN.

Row 17 Work K1, P1 Rib to 4 sts before next marker (on Left Front), TURN.

Row 18 Work K1, P1 Rib to end.

Row 19 Work K1, P1 Rib.

Row 20 Work K1, P1 Rib to 2 sts before 2nd marker (on Right Front), TURN.

Row 21 Work K1, P1 Rib to 2 sts before next marker (on Left Front), TURN.

Row 22 Work K1, P1 Rib to end.

Row 23 Work K1, P1 Rib.

Row 24 Work K1, P1 Rib to 2nd marker (on Right Front), TURN.

Row 25 Work K1, P1 Rib to next marker (on Left Front), TURN.

Row 26 Work K1, P1 Rib to end.

Bind off in rib.

Sew in Sleeves. Sew Sleeve and side seams.

Sew Pocket Linings to WS of Fronts.

Weave in ends. •

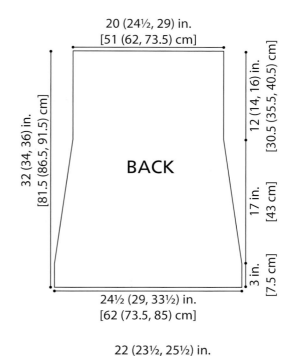

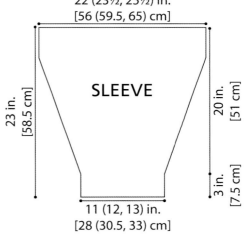

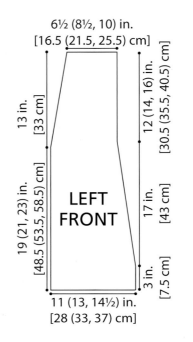

Effortless Cardigan

Intermediate

SIZES
XS (S, M, L, 1X).

MEASUREMENTS
Finished Bust (without front bands) 34 (38½, 42, 45½, 49½)"/ 86.5 (98, 106.5, 115.5, 125.5)cm
Finished Length 24¼ (26¼, 26¼, 26¼, 26¼)"/61.5 (66.5, 66.5, 66.5, 66.5)cm

MATERIALS
YARN
LION BRAND® Basic Stitch Premium™, 3½oz/100g balls, each approx 219yd/200m (acrylic)
• 4 (5, 5, 6, 6) balls in #150 Slate

NEEDLES
• One size 7 (4.5mm) circular knitting needle, 29"/73.5cm long, *or size to obtain gauge*

NOTIONS
• Stitch markers
• Stitch holders
• Tapestry needle

GAUGE
18 sts + 24 rows = approx 4"/10cm in St st.
BE SURE TO CHECK YOUR GAUGE.

K2, P2 RIB
(multiple of 4 sts plus 8)
Row 1 (RS) K3, *k2, p2; rep from * to last 5 sts, p2, k3.
Row 2 K the knit sts and p the purl sts.
Rep Row 2 for K2, P2 Rib.

NOTES
1) Cardigan is worked in one piece from the neck downwards.
2) Piece is divided at the underarms then body and sleeves are worked separately.
3) A circular needle is used to accommodate the number of stitches. Work back and forth in rows on circular needle as if working with straight needles.

CARDIGAN
YOKE
Cast on 48 (50, 56, 60, 64) sts.
Set-up Row 1 (RS) K2 for Left Front, pm, k8 for Left Sleeve, pm, k28 (30, 36, 40, 44) for Back, pm, k8 for Right Sleeve, pm, k2 for Right Front.
Row 2 Purl.
Raglan Inc Row 3 K1, *k to 1 st before next marker, kfb, sm, kfb; rep from * 3 more times, k to end of row—56 (58, 64, 68, 72) sts.
Rows 4 and 5 Rep Rows 2 and 3—64 (66, 72, 76, 80) sts.
Row 6 Purl.
Front Neck and Raglan Inc Row 7 K1, kfb, *k to 1 st before next marker, kfb, sm, kfb; rep from * 3 more times, k to last 3 sts, kfb, k2—74 (76, 82, 86, 90) sts.
Rep Rows 4–7 for 9 (11, 12, 13, 14) more times—236 (274, 298, 320, 342) sts.
Rep Rows 4 and 5 for 1 (1, 1, 1, 2) more time(s)—244 (282, 306, 328, 358) sts. Purl one row.

DIVIDE FOR BODY AND SLEEVES
K to marker, remove marker, place next 52 (60, 64, 68, 74) sts on holder for Left Sleeve, cast on 6 sts for underarm, remove next marker, k to next marker, remove marker, place next 52 (60, 64, 68, 74) sts on holder for Right Sleeve, cast on 6 sts for underarm, remove next marker, k to end—152 (174, 190, 204, 222) sts rem for body.

Effortless Cardigan

BODY

Work even in St st (k on RS, p on WS) until piece measures approx 21½ (23½, 23½, 23½, 23½)"/54.5 (59.5, 59.5, 59.5, 59.5)cm from beg or approx 2¾"/7cm less than desired final length, end with RS row as last row you work.

Inc Row (WS) Purl, working 0 (2, 2, 0, 2) increases (pfb) evenly across—152 (176, 192, 204, 224) sts.

Lower ribbing

Work K2, P2 Rib for 2¾"/7cm, end with a WS row as last row you work.

Bind off in rib on RS.

SLEEVES

Row 1 (RS) Cast on 1 st; from RS, beg at center of one underarm, pick up and k 3 sts evenly along cast-on sts of underarm, k52 (60, 64, 68, 74) sts from st holder, pick up and k 3 sts evenly spaced along rem cast-on sts of underarm, cast on 1 st—60 (68, 72, 76, 82) sts.

Work even in St st for 6 (4, 4, 4, 6) rows.

Dec Row K2, ssk, k to last 4 sts, k2tog, k2—58 (66, 70, 74, 80) sts.

Work even in St st for 11 (11, 9, 9, 7) rows.

Rep Dec Row—56 (64, 68, 72, 78) sts.

Rep last 12 (12, 10, 10, 8) rows 5 (5, 7, 7, 8) more times—46 (54, 54, 58, 62) sts.

Work even in St st for 12 (12, 6, 4, 10) rows or until sleeve measures approx 2¾"/7cm less than desired sleeve length, end with a RS row as last row you work.

Next Row (WS) Purl, working 10 decreases (p2tog) evenly across—36 (44, 44, 48, 52) sts.

Wrist ribbing

Work in K2, P2 Rib for 2¾"/7cm, end with a WS row as last row you work.

Bind off in rib on RS.

Rep for 2nd sleeve.

POCKETS

Cast on 28 sts.

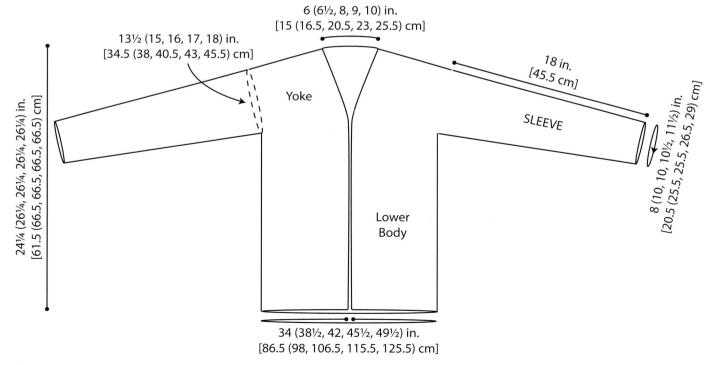

Work even in St st until piece measures approx 5"/12.5cm from beg, end with a WS row as last row you work.

Next Row K3, *k2, p2; rep from * to last 5 sts, k5.

Next 5 rows K the knit sts and p the purl sts. Bind off loosely in rib on RS.

FINISHING
Front and neck bands

With RS facing, beg at lower Right Front edge, pick up and k 2 sts for every 3 rows along Right Front edge, across Back neck, and down Left Front edge. Adjust number of sts picked up, if necessary, so you have a multiple of 4 sts.

Next Row (WS) P3, *k2, p2; rep from * to last 5 sts, k2, p3.

Next Row K the knit sts and p the purl sts. Rep last row for 2"/5cm, end with a WS row as last row you work.

Bind off loosely in rib.

Sew sleeve and underarm seams.
Sew a pocket to each front, just above ribbing and 2 sts from front band.

Weave in ends. •

Comfy Striped Cardigan

Easy

SIZES
XS/S (M/L, 1X/2X, 3X/4X).

MEASUREMENTS
Finished Bust (with front bands) 43½ (47, 50½, 54)"/ 110.5 (119.5, 128.5, 137)cm
Finished Length 24 (24½, 25, 25½)"/61 (62, 63.5, 65)cm

MATERIALS
YARN
LION BRAND® Wool-Ease® Thick & Quick®, 6oz/170g balls, each approx 106yd/97m (acrylic/wool)
- 3 (3, 4, 4) balls in #137 Terracotta (A)
- 2 (3, 3, 4) balls in #127 Peanut (B)
- 1 (2, 2, 2) balls in #099 Fisherman (C)

NEEDLES
- One size 13 (9mm) circular knitting needle, 40"/101.5cm long, *or size to obtain gauge*

NOTIONS
- Stitch holders
- Tapestry needle

GAUGE
9 sts = approx 4"/10cm and 14 rows = approx 5"/12.5cm in St st.
BE SURE TO CHECK YOUR GAUGE.

NOTES
1) Cardigan is made in 3 pieces: Body and 2 Sleeves.
2) Body is worked from lower edge upwards. Piece is divided at underarms then fronts and back are worked separately up to shoulders. Sleeves are worked separately.
3) Yarn color is changed following Stripe Sequences. When changing yarn color, do not cut old color if it will be used again in a few rows. This will reduce the number of yarn ends to weave in later.
4) A circular needle is used to accommodate the number of stitches. Work back and forth in rows on the circular needle as if working on straight needles.
5) The band is worked from stitches picked up along front and neck edges.

BODY STRIPE SEQUENCE
Work *2 rows with B, 2 rows with A, [2 rows with B, 2 rows with C] twice, 2 rows with A, 2 rows with B, 2 rows with A, 2 rows with C, 2 rows with B, 2 rows with C; rep from * for Body Stripe Sequence.

SLEEVE STRIPE SEQUENCE
Work *4 rows with B, 2 rows with C, 4 rows with B, 2 rows with A, 4 rows with C, 2 rows with B, 4 rows with C, 2 rows with A; rep from * for Sleeve Stripe Sequence.

CARDIGAN
BODY
With A, cast on 109 (117, 125, 133) sts.
Row 1 (WS) With A, k1, *p1, k1; rep from * to end.
Row 2 With B, knit.
Row 3 With B, k1, *p1, k1; rep from * to end.
Rows 4 and 5 With A, rep Rows 2 and 3.

Begin body stripe sequence
Note Begin body stripe sequence and continue with it to end of all sections of body.
Rows 1 and 2 With B, beg with a RS row, work in St st (k on RS, p on WS).
Dec Row 3 (RS) With A, k1, k2tog, k to last 3 sts, ssk, k1—107 (115, 123, 131) sts.
Row 4 With A, purl.

Comfy Striped Cardigan

Rep Rows 1–4 for 9 more times following Body Stripe Sequence—89 (97, 105, 113) sts.

Divide for fronts and back

Next Row (RS) Knit.
Next Row (WS) P18 (20, 21, 23) and place these sts on a holder for left front, bind off 6 (6, 8, 8) sts for armhole, p until there are 41 (45, 47, 51) sts on right needle and place these sts on a holder for back, bind off 6 (6, 8, 8) sts for 2nd armhole, p to end for right front—18 (20, 21, 23) sts rem on needle for right front.

Right front

Dec Row 1 (RS) K1, k2tog, k to end—17 (19, 20, 22) sts.
Rows 2–4 Work even in St st.
Dec Row 5 Rep Dec Row 1—16 (18, 19, 21) sts.
Rep rows 2–5 until 13 (14, 15, 16) sts rem.
Work even in St st until Right Front measures approx 7½ (8, 8½, 9)"/19 (20.5, 21.5, 23)cm from divide, end with a WS row as last row you work.
Bind off.

Back

Return 41 (45, 47, 51) Back sts to needle, ready to work a RS row.
Work even in St st until Back measures same as Right Front, end with same stripe as on Right Front.
Bind off.

Left front

Return 18 (20, 21, 23) Left Front sts to needle, ready to work a RS row.
Dec Row 1 (RS) K to last 3 sts, ssk, k1—17 (19, 20, 22) sts.
Rows 2–4 Work even in St st.
Dec Row 5 Rep Dec Row 1—16 (18, 19, 21) sts.
Rep rows 2–5 until 13 (14, 15, 16) sts rem.
Work even in St st until Left Front measures same as Back, ending with same stripe as on back.
Bind off.

SLEEVES

With A, cast on 23 (25, 27, 29) sts.
Row 1 (WS) With A, k1, *p1, k1; rep from * to end.
Row 2 With B, knit.
Row 3 With B, k1, *p1, k1; rep from * to end.
Rows 4 and 5 With A, rep Rows 2 and 3.

Begin sleeve stripe sequence

Note Begin sleeve stripe sequence and continue with it to end of sleeve.
Rows 1 and 2 With B, beg with a RS row, work in St st for 2 rows
Inc Row 3 (RS) With B, k1, M1, k to last st, M1, k1—25 (27, 29, 31) sts.
Row 4 With B, purl.
Rows 5 and 6 With C, work in St st for 2 rows.
Rows 7–10 With B, work in St st for 4 rows.
Row 11 With A, rep Inc Row 3—27 (29, 31, 33) sts.
Rep Rows 4–11 for 4 more times following Sleeve Stripe Sequence—35 (37, 39, 41) sts.
Work even in St st and continue to change yarn color following Sleeve Stripe Sequence until piece measures approx 22"/56cm from beg.
Bind off.

FINISHING

Sew shoulder seams.

Front Bands

Pick-up Row (RS) With A and RS facing, beg at lower Right Front corner, pick up and k 1 st in end of each row up Right Front edge to shoulder seam, pick up and k 15 (17, 17, 19) sts along Back neck, pick up and k same number of sts down Left Front edge as were picked up along Right Front edge.
Row 1 (WS) With A, k1, *p1, k1; rep from * to end of row.
Row 2 With B, knit.
Row 3 With B, k1, *p1, k1; rep from * to end.

Rows 4 and 5 With A, rep Rows 2 and 3.
Bind off.

Sew Sleeve seams.
Sew Sleeves into armholes.
Weave in ends. •

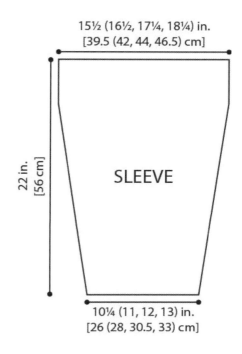

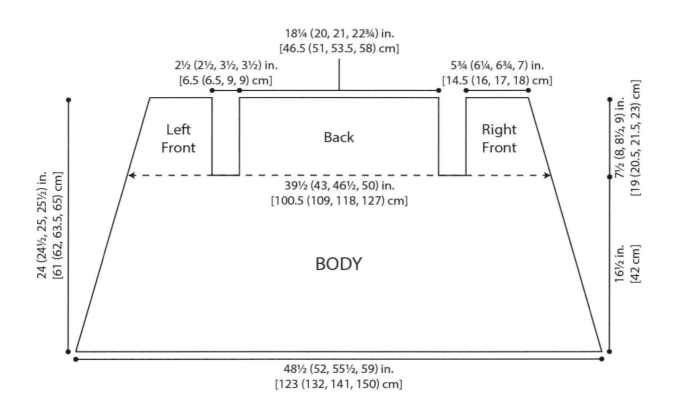

Birger Cardigan

Easy

SIZES
XS/S (M/L, 1X/2X).

MEASUREMENTS
Finished Bust (fronts overlapped) 44 (52, 60)"/112 (132, 152.5)cm

Finished Length 23 (24, 25)"/58.5 (61, 63.5)cm

MATERIALS
YARN

LION BRAND® Hometown®, 5oz/142g balls, each approx 81yd/74m (acrylic)

- 7 (9, 11) balls in #218 Bar Harbor Blizzard (A)
- 3 (4, 5) balls in #150 Chicago Charcoal (B)

NEEDLES

- One size 11 (8mm) circular knitting needle, 29"/73.5cm long, *or size to obtain gauge*

NOTIONS

- Stitch markers
- Tapestry needle

GAUGE
13 sts = approx 5½"/14cm and 13 rows = approx 4½"/11.5cm in St st.
BE SURE TO CHECK YOUR GAUGE.

NOTES
1) Cardigan is worked in 5 pieces: Back, 2 Fronts, and 2 Sleeves.
2) Each piece is worked in Stockinette stitch with 2 colors of yarn.
3) Front bands are worked in garter stitch in one with each Front.
4) Simple embroidery is worked on completed pieces.
5) Cardigan is designed without a neck band.
6) A circular needle is used to accommodate the number of stitches. Work back and forth in rows on the circular needle as if working on straight needles.

STRIPE SEQUENCE
Row 1 (RS) With B, knit.
Rows 2–6 With B, continue in St st.
Rows 7–16 With A, work in St st.
Rep Rows 1–16 for Stripe Sequence.

CARDIGAN
BACK

With A, cast on 52 (62, 71) sts.
Edging Row (WS) Knit.
Beg with a RS row, work in St st (k on RS, p on WS) with A for 6 row, ending with a WS row.
Beginning with Row 1, work in Stripe Sequence until piece measures about 21½ (22½, 23½)"/54.5 (57, 59.5)cm from beg, end with a Row 6, 8, 10, 12, 14 or 16 of Stripe Sequence as last row you work.
The last row you worked will have been a WS (purl) row. Change to A, and continue with A only for remainder of Back.

Shape shoulders
Row 1 (RS) Bind off 6 (8, 10) sts, k to end—46 (54, 61) sts.
Row 2 Bind off 6 (8, 10) sts, p to end—40 (46, 51) sts.

Shape neck, continue shaping shoulders
Place a marker on each side of center 12 (14, 15) sts.
Row 3 (RS) Bind off 7 (8, 9) sts, k to marker for right shoulder; join a 2nd ball of yarn and bind off center 12 (14, 15) sts, k to end of row for left shoulder—7 (8, 9) sts for right shoulder and 14 (16, 18) sts for left shoulder.

Birger Cardigan

Work both shoulders AT THE SAME TIME with separate balls of yarn as follows:
Row 4 On left shoulder, bind off 7 (8, 9) sts, p to end of side; on right shoulder, p to end of side—7 (8, 9) sts for each shoulder.
Row 5 On right shoulder, bind off rem 7 (8, 9) sts; on left shoulder, k to end of side.
Bind off rem 7 (8, 9) sts of left shoulder.

LEFT FRONT
With A, cast on 33 (38, 43) sts.
Edging Row (WS) Knit.
Row 1 (RS) Knit.
Row 2 K3 for front band, p to end of row.
Rows 3–6 Rep Rows 1 and 2.
Keeping 3 front band sts in garter st (k every st on every row) and beg with Row 1, work in Stripe Sequence until piece measures approx 18 (19, 20)"/45.5 (48.5, 51)cm from beg, end with any RS row of Stripe Sequence except Row 7 or 9.
Note It is important to end with a specific RS row here to ensure that the Stripe Sequence continues to flow smoothly through the shaping that follows.

Shape neck
Continue in Stripe Sequence as follows:
Row 1 (WS) Bind off 7 (8, 8) sts, p to end of row—26 (30, 35) sts.
Rows 2, 4, and 6 Knit.
Row 3 Bind off 3 (3, 4) sts, p to end—23 (27, 31) sts.
Row 5 Bind off 2 sts, p to end—21 (25, 29) sts.
Row 7 Bind off 1 st, p to end—20 (24, 28) sts.
Rows 8–11 Work even in St st.
Change to A, and continue with A only for remainder of Left Front.

Shape shoulder
Row 12 (RS) Bind off 6 (8, 10) sts, k to end—14 (16, 18) sts.
Row 13 Purl.
Row 14 Bind off 7 (8, 9) sts, k to end—7 (8, 9) sts.
Row 15 Purl.
Bind off rem 7 (8, 9) sts.

RIGHT FRONT
With A, cast on 33 (38, 43) sts.
Edging Row (WS) Knit.
Row 1 (RS) Knit.
Row 2 P to last 3 sts, k3 for front band.
Rows 3–6 Rep Rows 1 and 2.
Keeping 3 front band sts in garter st and beg with Row 1, work in Stripe Sequence until piece measures same as Left Front to neck shaping, end with any WS row of Stripe Sequence except Row 6, 8, or 10.

Shape neck
Continue in Stripe Sequence as follows:
Row 1 (RS) Bind off 7 (8, 8) sts, k to end—26 (30, 35) sts.
Rows 2, 4, and 6 Purl.
Row 3 Bind off 3 (3, 4) sts, k to end—23 (27, 31) sts.
Row 5 Bind off 2 sts, k to end—21 (25, 29) sts.
Row 7 Bind off 1 st, k to end—20 (24, 28) sts.
Rows 8–11 Work even in St st.
Change to A, and continue with A only for remainder of Right Front.

Shape shoulder
Row 12 (WS) Bind off 6 (8, 10) sts, p to end—14 (16, 18) sts.
Row 13 Knit.
Row 14 Bind off 7 (8, 9) sts, p to end—7 (8, 9) sts.
Row 15 Purl.
Bind off rem 7 (8, 9) sts.

SLEEVES

With A, cast on 19 (21, 24) sts.

Edging Row (WS) Knit.

Inc Row 1 (RS) With A, k1, M1, k to last st, M1, k1—21 (23, 26) sts.

Rows 2–6 With A, work in St st.

Beg with Row 1, work in Stripe Sequence, AT THE SAME TIME shape Sleeve as follows:

Inc Row 7 Rep Inc Row 1—23 (25, 28) sts.

Rows 8–12 Work in St st.

Inc Row 13 Rep Inc Row 1—25 (27, 30) sts.

Rows 14–16 Work in St st.

Row 17 Rep Inc Row 1—27 (29, 32) sts.

Rows 18–20 Work in St st.

Inc Row 21 Rep Inc Row 1—29 (31, 35) sts.

Row 22 Purl.

Rep Rows 7–22, then rep Rows 7–12 (7–16, 7–20) once more—39 (43, 48) sts.

Continue in St st and Stripe Sequence until piece measures approx 19"/48.5cm from beg, end with a Row 6, 8, 10, 12, 14, or 16 of Stripe Sequence as last row you work.

Shape cap

Change to A, and continue with A only.

Row 1 (RS) Bind off 7 (8, 9) sts, k to end—32 (35, 39) sts.

Row 2 Bind off 7 (8, 9) sts, p to end—25 (27, 30) sts.

Rows 3 and 4 Rep Rows 1 and 2—11 (11, 12) sts.

Bind off rem 11 (11, 12) sts.

FINISHING

Embroidery

With A, embroider 2 lines of straight sts, spaced over and under 2 St sts, along every B-colored stripe.

Sew shoulder seams.

Place markers on side edges of Back and Fronts, approx 8 (9, 10)"/20.5 (23, 25.5)cm below shoulder seams. Sew tops of Sleeves between markers.

Sew side and Sleeve seams.

Weave in ends. •

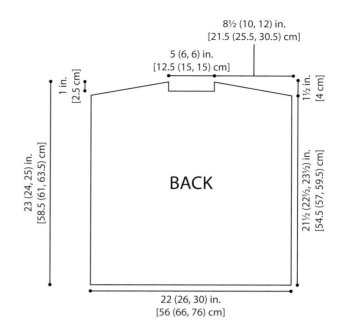

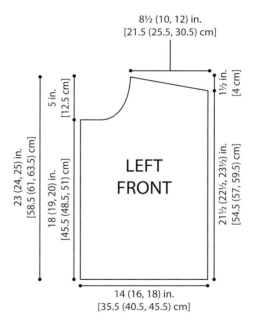

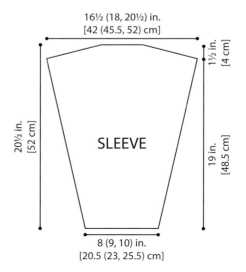

Clusterwell Cardigan

Intermediate

SIZES
S (M, L, 1X, 2X).

MEASUREMENTS
Finished Bust 33½ (37, 40½, 44, 47½)"/85 (94, 103, 112, 120.5)cm
Finished Length 21 (22, 22, 22 ½, 23)"/53.5 (56, 56, 57, 58.5)cm

MATERIALS
YARN
LION BRAND® Wool-Ease® Thick & Quick®, 6oz/170g balls, each approx 106yd/97m (acrylic/wool)
- 6 (7, 7, 8, 9) balls in #147 Eggplant

NEEDLES
- One size 13 (9mm) circular knitting needle, 29"/73.5cm long, *or size to obtain gauge*
- One pair size 11 (8mm) knitting needles

NOTIONS
- Stitch markers and holders
- Cable needle (cn)
- Tapestry needle

GAUGE
- 8 sts = approx 3½"/9cm and 12 rows = approx 4"/10cm in garter st using larger needle.
BE SURE TO CHECK YOUR GAUGE.

STITCH GLOSSARY
5/5 LC (5 over 5 left cross) Sl 5 sts to cn and hold in front, k5, then k5 from cn.
5/5 RC (5 over 5 right cross) Sl 5 sts to cn and hold in back, k5, then k5 from cn.

CABLE I
(over 15 sts)
Rows 1–4 Work in St st for 4 rows.
Row 5 (RS) 5/5 LC, k5.
Rows 6–12 Work in St st for 7 rows.
Row 13 K5, 5/5 RC.
Rows 14–20 Work in St st for 7 rows.
Rep Rows 5–20 for Cable I pattern.

CABLE II
(over 15 sts)
Rows 1–4 Work in St st for 4 rows.
Row 5 (RS) K5, 5/5 RC.
Rows 6–12 Work in St st for 7 rows.
Row 13 5/5 LC, k5.
Rows 14–20 Work in St st for 7 rows.
Rep Rows 5–20 for Cable II pattern.

K1, P1 RIB
(over an odd number of sts)
Row 1 K1, *p1, k1; rep from * to end of row.
Row 2 K the knit sts and p the purl sts.
Rep Row 2 for K1, P1 Rib.

NOTES
1) Cardigan is worked in 3 pieces: Body and 2 Sleeves.
2) Cable patterns are worked along fronts and sleeves. Right and Left Sleeve are shaped identically but each uses a different Cable pattern.
3) The large circular needle is used to accommodate the large number of stitches. Work back and forth in rows on the circular needle as if working on straight needles.
4) Use the smaller straight needles for Sleeve ribbing only.
5) Cable patterns can be worked following written instructions or reading charts.

Clusterwell Cardigan

CARDIGAN

BODY

With circular needle, cast on 86 (94, 102, 110, 118) sts.

Set-Up Row (WS) K5 (6, 6, 7, 7), pm, p15, pm, k46 (52, 60, 66, 74), pm, p15, pm, k5 (6, 6, 7, 7).

Row 1 (RS) K to marker, sm, work Row 1 of Cable I pat, sm, k to next marker, sm, work Row 1 of Cable II pat, sm, k to end.

Row 2 K to first marker, sm, work Row 2 of Cable II pattern, sm, k to next marker, sm, work Row 2 of Cable I pattern, sm, k to end of row.

Continue in Garter st (k every st on every row), slipping markers as you come to them, and working Cable patterns between markers for 37 more rows, end with a Row 7 of Cable patterns as last row you work.

Divide for armholes

Next Row (WS) K to marker, sm, work Cable II pattern as established to next marker, sm, k3 (4, 6, 7, 9), place these 23 (25, 27, 29, 31) sts onto holder for left front; bind off next 4 sts for underarm, k until there are 32 (36, 40, 44, 48) sts on right needle and place these sts onto 2nd holder for back; bind off next 4 sts for underarm, k to marker, sm, work Cable I pattern as established to next marker, sm, k to end—23 (25, 27, 29, 31) sts rem on needle for right front.

Right front

Work over right front sts only as follows:

SHAPE ARMHOLE

Row 1 (RS) K to marker, sm, work Cable I pattern to next marker, sm, k to last 3 sts, k2tog, k1—22 (24, 26, 28, 30) sts.

Row 2 Work even in patterns.

Row 3 K to marker, sm, work Cable I pattern to next marker, sm, k to last 2 (3, 3, 3, 3) sts, k2tog, k0 (1, 1, 1, 1)—21 (23, 25, 27, 29) sts.

Rows 4–18 Work even in patterns.

SHAPE NECK

Row 1 (RS) Bind off 7 (8, 9, 10, 10) sts and remove first marker, work in patterns as established to end—14 (15, 16, 17, 19) sts.

Rows 2 and 3 Work even in patterns.

Row 4 K to marker, sm, p to last 2 sts, p2tog tbl—13 (14, 15, 16, 18) sts.

Row 5 Work even in patterns.

Rep Rows 4 and 5 for 0 (1, 1, 1, 1) more time(s)—13 (13, 14, 15, 17) sts.

Work even in patterns for 0 (0, 0, 2, 4) rows.

Bind off rem 13 (13, 14, 15, 17) sts.

Left front

Return 23 (25, 27, 29, 31) left front sts to larger needle, ready to work a RS row.

SHAPE ARMHOLE

Row 1 (RS) K1, ssk, k to marker, sm, work Cable II pattern to marker, sm, k to end—22 (24, 26, 28, 30) sts.

Row 2 Work even in patterns.

Row 3 K0 (1, 1, 1, 1), ssk, k to marker, sm, work Cable II pattern to next marker, sm, k to end—21 (23, 25, 27, 29) sts.

Rows 4–19 Work even in patterns.

SHAPE NECK

Row 1 (WS) Bind off 7 (8, 9, 10, 10) sts and remove first marker, work in patterns as established to end—14 (15, 16, 17, 19) sts.

Row 2 Work even in patterns.

Row 3 P2tog, p to marker, sm, k to end—13 (14, 15, 16, 18) sts.

Row 4 Work even in patterns.

Rep Rows 3 and 4 for 0 (1, 1, 1, 1) more time(s)—13 (13, 14, 15, 17) sts.

Work even in patterns for 0 (0, 0, 2, 4) rows.

Bind off rem 13 (13, 14, 15, 17) sts.

Back

Return 32 (36, 40, 44, 48) back sts to larger needle, ready to work a RS row.

SHAPE ARMHOLE

Row 1 (RS) K1, ssk, k to last 3 sts, k2tog, k1—30 (34, 38, 42, 46) sts.
Row 2 Knit.
Rep Rows 1 and 2 once—28 (32, 36, 40, 44) sts.
Work even in garter st until back measures same as fronts. Bind off.

RIGHT SLEEVE

With straight needles, cast on 25 (25, 27, 27, 29) sts.
Work in K1, P1 Rib until piece measures approx 3"/7.5cm from beg.
Change to circular needle and work back and forth in rows.
Set-up Row (WS) K5 (5, 6, 6, 7), pm, p15, pm, k to end.
Row 1 K to marker, sm, work Row 1 of Cable II pattern to marker, sm, k to end.
Row 2 K to marker, sm, work Row 2 of Cable II pattern to marker, sm, k to end.
Rows 3–18 Work even in patterns.
Row 19 (RS) K1, M1, k to marker, sm, work Cable II pattern to marker, sm, k to last st, M1, k1—27 (27, 29, 29, 31) sts.
Rows 20–24 Work even in patterns.
Row 25 K1, M1, k to marker, sm, work Cable II pattern to marker, sm, k to last st, M1, k1—2 sts increased.
Rep Rows 20–25 for 2 (3, 3, 4, 4) more times—33 (35, 37, 39, 41).
Work even in patterns until piece measures approx 19"/48.5cm from beg, end with a WS row as last row you work.

Shape cap

Rows 1 and 2 Bind off 2 sts, work in patterns to end—29 (31, 33, 35, 37) sts.
Row 3 (RS) K1, ssk, work in patterns to last 3 sts, k2tog, k1—27 (29, 31, 33, 35) sts.
Row 4 Work even in patterns.
Row 5 Rep Row 3—25 (27, 29, 31, 33) sts.
Bind off.

LEFT SLEEVE

Work same as for Right Sleeve, except work Cable Pattern 1 between markers.

FINISHING

Place markers on each side of center 12 (14, 16, 18, 20) sts of back for back neck. Sew shoulder seams, sewing from outer edge to markers, easing front shoulders to fit and allowing front edge fabric to roll under slightly. Sew Sleeve seams. Sew in Sleeves.

Clusterwell Cardigan

Collar

Row 1 (RS) With RS facing and circular needle, skip first 5 sts of right front neck shaping, then pick up and k 8 (9, 10, 11, 11) sts evenly along rem right front neck edge, 15 (15, 17, 19, 19) sts along back neck, and 8 (9, 10, 11, 11) sts evenly along left front neck edge to last 5 sts—31 (33, 37, 41, 41) sts.

Rows 2–7 Knit.

Row 8 [K5 (5, 5, 6, 6), M1] 5 (5, 6, 6, 6) times, k to end—36 (38, 43, 47, 47) sts.

Rows 9–14 knit.

Bind off.

Weave in ends. •

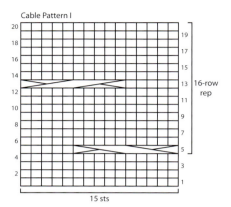

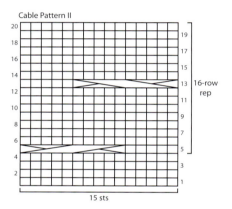

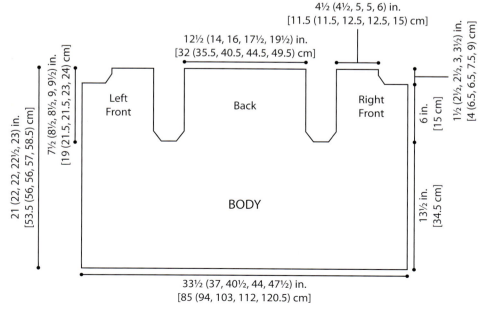

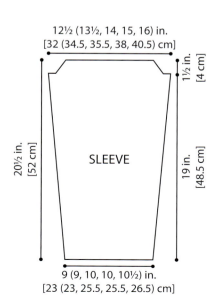

Emelio Cardigan

Intermediate

SIZES
S (M, L, 1X).

MEASUREMENTS
Finished Bust 39 (43, 47, 51)"/99 (109, 119.5, 129.5)cm
Finished Length 26 (26½, 27, 27½)"/66 (67.5, 68.5, 70)cm

MATERIALS
YARN
LION BRAND® Basic Stitch Anti-Pilling™, 3½oz/100g balls, each approx 185yd/170m (acrylic)
- 6 (7, 8, 9) balls in #123 Cedarwood

NEEDLES
- One pair size 7 (4.5mm) knitting needles, *or size to obtain gauge*

NOTIONS
- Stitch markers
- Tapestry needle

GAUGE
22 sts + 24 rows = approx 4"/10cm in Sailor Rib.
BE SURE TO CHECK YOUR GAUGE.

LOWER BAND PATTERN
Row 1 (RS) Purl.
Rows 2 and 3 Knit.
Rows 4–6 Work in K1, P1 Rib for 3 rows.
Rows 7 and 8 Knit.

SAILOR RIB
(multiple of 5 sts plus 1)
Row 1 (RS) K1 tbl, *p1, k2, p1, k1 tbl; rep from * to end.
Row 2 P1, *k1, p2, k1, p1; rep from * to end.
Row 3 K1 tbl, *p4, k1 tbl; rep from * to end.
Row 4 P1, *k4, p1; rep from * to end.
Rep Rows 1–4 for Sailor Rib.

K1, P1 RIB
(over an even number of sts)
Row 1 *K1, p1; rep from * to end.
Row 2 K the knit sts and p the purl sts.
Rep Row 2 for K1, P1 Rib.

K1, P1 RIB
(over an odd number of sts)
Row 1 K1, *p1, k1; rep from * to end.
Row 2 K the knit sts and p the purl sts.
Rep Row 2 for K1, P1 Rib.

Emelio Cardigan

SLIP STITCH RIB

(over 12 sts)

Row 1 (RS) [P2, k1, sl 1 wyib, k1] twice, p2.

Row 2 [K2, p3] twice, k2.

Rep Rows 1 and 2 for Slip Stitch Rib.

NOTES

1) Cardigan is made in 5 pieces: Back, 2 Fronts, and 2 Sleeves.

2) Selvedge stitches will be hidden in the seams when pieces are sewn together.

CARDIGAN

BACK

Cast on 108 (118, 128, 138) sts.

Work Rows 1–8 of Lower Band pattern.

Row 1 (RS) Sl 1 (selvedge st), work Row 1 of Sailor Rib to last st, p1 (selvedge st).

Row 2 Sl 1, work next row of Sailor Rib pattern to last st, p1.

Continue in Sailor Rib pattern as established, slipping first st and purling last st for selvedges, until piece measures approx 23½ (24, 24½, 25)"/59.5 (61, 62, 63.5)cm from beg, end with a WS row as last row you work.

Shape shoulders

Next 10 (6, 2, 8) Rows Bind off 3 (4, 4, 5) sts, work in pattern to end—78 (94, 120, 98) sts.

Next 2 (6, 10, 4) Rows Bind off 4 (4, 5, 6) sts, work in pattern to end—70 (70, 70, 74) sts.

Shape neck and shoulders

Place marker on each side of center 40 (40, 38, 40) sts.

Row 1 (RS) Bind off 4 (4, 5, 6) sts, work in pattern to first marker for right side of neck, join 2nd ball of yarn and bind off sts between markers for back neck and remove markers, work pattern to end of row for left side of neck—11 sts for right side and 15 (15, 16, 17) sts for left side.

Note Work both sides of neck AT THE SAME TIME using separate balls of yarn.

Row 2 On left side, bind off 4 (4, 5, 6) sts, work in pattern to end of side; on right side, bind off 2 sts, work in pattern to end of side—9 sts for right side and 11 sts for left side.

Row 3 On right side, bind off rem 9 sts; on left side, bind off 2 sts, work pattern to end of side—9 sts rem on left side.

Bind off rem 9 sts of left side.

LEFT FRONT

Cast on 55 (60, 65, 75) sts.

Row 1 (RS) Work Row 1 of Lower Band pattern to last 13 sts, pm, work Row 1 of Slip Stitch Rib over next 12 sts (for front band), p1 (selvedge st).

Row 2 Sl 1 (selvedge st), work next row of Slip Stitch Rib to marker, sm, work next row of Lower Band pattern to end of row.

Continue in patterns as established until all 8 rows of Lower Band pattern have been worked.

Body

Row 1 (RS) Sl 1, work Row 1 of Sailor Rib to marker, sm, work Slip Stitch Rib to last st, p1.

Row 2 Sl 1, work Slip Stitch Rib to marker, sm, work Sailor Rib to last st, p1.

Continue in patterns as established until piece measures approx 11 (11½, 11½, 12)"/28 (29, 29, 30.5)cm from beg, end with a WS row as last row you work.

Shape neck

Dec Row 1 (RS) Sl 1, work Sailor Rib to 2 sts before marker, k2tog, sm, work Slip Stitch Rib to last st, p1—54 (59, 64, 74) sts.

Continue in patterns as established for 7 (7, 7, 5) rows. Rep last 8 (8, 8, 6) rows 9 (9, 8, 14) more times and AT THE SAME TIME when piece measures approx 23½ (24, 24½, 25)"/59.5 (61, 62, 63.5)cm from beg, end with a

WS row and beg Shape Shoulder (following instructions below) and continue to work any rem neck decreases.

Shape shoulder

Row 1 (RS) Bind off 3 (4, 4, 5) sts, work Sailor Rib to marker (if not all neck decreases have been completed, work k2tog in last 2 sts before marker), sm, work Slip Stitch Rib to last st, p1.
Row 2 Sl 1, work Slip Stitch Rib to marker, sm, work Sailor Rib to last st, p1.
Rep Rows 1 and 2 for 4 (2, 0, 3) more times.

Next Row (RS) Bind off 4 (4, 5, 6) sts, work Sailor Rib to marker (if not all neck decreases have been completed, work k2tog in last 2 sts before marker), sm, work Slip Stitch Rib to last st, p1.
Next Row Sl 1, work Slip Stitch Rib to marker, sm, work Sailor Rib to last st, p1.
Rep last 2 rows for 1 (3, 5, 2) more times, removing marker as you work last bind-off row.

Next Row Bind off 9 sts, remove marker, work in Slip Stitch Rib to last st, p1—13 sts.
Next Row Sl 1, work Slip Stitch Rib to marker, sm, work Sailor Rib to last st, p1.

Collar extension

Row 1 (RS) Work Slip Stitch Rib to last st, p1.
Row 2 Sl 1, work Slip Stitch Rib to end.
Work even in Slip Stitch Rib until collar extension measures long enough to reach center of back neck.
Bind off.

RIGHT FRONT

Cast on 55 (60, 65, 75) sts.
Row 1 (RS) Sl 1 (selvedge st), work Row 1 of Slip Stitch Rib over next 12 sts (for front band), pm, work Row 1 of Lower Band pattern to end of row.
Row 2 Work next row of Lower Band pattern to marker, sm, work next row of Slip Stitch Rib to last st, p1 (selvedge).
Continue in patterns as established until all 8 rows of Lower Band pattern have been worked.

Emelio Cardigan

Body

Row 1 (RS) Sl 1, work Slip Stitch Rib to marker, sm, work Row 1 of Sailor Rib to last st, p1.

Row 2 Sl 1, work next row of Sailor Rib to marker, sm, work Slip Stitch Rib to last st, p1.

Continue in patterns as established until piece measures approx 11 (11½, 11½, 12, 12)"/28 (29, 29, 30.5)cm from beg, end with a WS row as last row you work.

Shape neck

Dec Row 1 (RS) Sl 1, work Slip Stitch Rib to marker, sm, ssk, work Sailor Rib to last st, p1—54 (59, 64, 74, 79, 84) sts.

Work in patterns as established for 7 (7, 7, 5) rows.

Rep last 8 (8, 8, 6) rows 9 (9, 8, 14) more times and AT THE SAME TIME when piece measures approx 23½ (24, 24½, 25)"/59.5 (61, 62, 63.5)cm from beg, end with a WS row and beg Shape Shoulder (following instructions below) and continue to work any rem neck decreases.

Shape shoulder

Row 1 (RS) Sl 1, work Slip Stitch Rib to marker, sm, (if not all neck decreases have been completed, work ssk here), work Sailor Rib to last st, p1.

Row 2 Bind off 3 (4, 4, 5) sts, work Sailor Rib to marker, sm, work Slip Stitch Rib to last st, p1.

Rep Rows 1 and 2 for 4 (2, 0, 3) more times.

Next Row (RS) Sl 1, work Slip Stitch Rib to marker, sm, (if not all neck decreases have been completed, work ssk here), work Sailor Rib to last st, p1.

Next Row Bind off 4 (4, 5, 6) sts, work Sailor Rib to marker, sm, work Slip Stitch Rib to last st, p1.

Rep last 2 rows for 1 (3, 5, 2) more times, removing marker as you work last bind-off row.

Next Row Sl 1, work Slip Stitch Rib to marker, sm, (if not all neck decreases have been completed, work ssk here), work Sailor Rib to last st, p1.

Next Row Bind off 9 sts, remove marker, work Slip Stitch Rib to last st, p1—13 sts.

Collar extension

Row 1 (RS) Sl 1, work Slip Stitch Rib to end.

Row 2 Work Slip Stitch Rib to last st, p1.

Work even in Slip Stitch Rib until collar extension measures long enough to reach center of back neck.
Bind off.

SLEEVES

Cast on 53 (53, 58, 58) sts.

Work rows 1–8 of Lower Band pattern.

Row 1 (RS) Sl 1 (selvedge st), work Row 1 of Sailor Rib to last st, p1 (selvedge st).

Row 2 Sl 1, work next row of Sailor Rib to last st, p1.

Inc Row (RS) Sl 1, M1, work Sailor Rib to last st, M1, p1—55 (55, 60, 60) sts.

Continue in Sailor Rib as established, slipping first st and purling last st for selvedges and working new sts into pattern for 5 (5, 5, 3) more row(s).

Rep Inc Row—57 (57, 62, 62) sts.

Rep last 6 (6, 6, 4) rows for 11 (13, 14, 17) more times—79 (83, 90, 96) sts.

Work even in Sailor Rib, slipping first st and purling last st for selvedges, until piece measures approx 17"/43cm from beg.

Shape cap

Next 4 (10, 12, 6) Rows Bind off 3 (4, 4, 4) sts, work Sailor Rib to end—67 (43, 42, 72) sts.

Next 14 (8, 6, 12) Rows Bind off 4 (4, 5, 5) sts, work Sailor Rib to end—11 (11, 12, 12) sts.
Bind off.

FINISHING

Sew shoulder seams.

Sew short ends of collar extensions together. Sew edge of collar extensions to back neck edge.

Place markers on side edges of Back and Fronts, approx 7½ (8, 8½, 9)"/19, 20.5, 21.5, 23)cm from shoulder seam.

Sew Sleeves between markers.

Sew side and Sleeve seams.

Weave in ends. Block to measurements. •

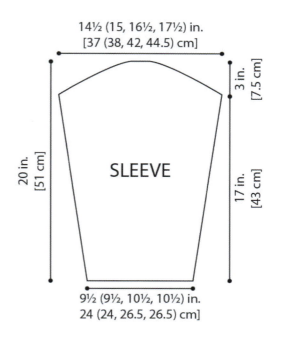

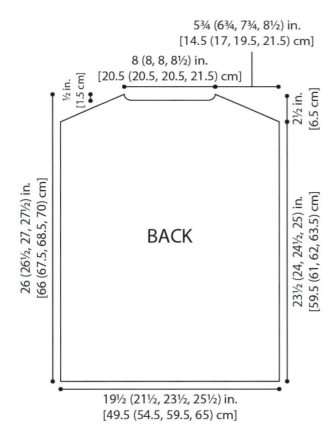

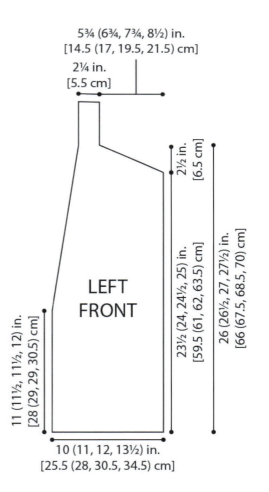

Drapey Cardigan

Intermediate

SIZES
XS/S (M/L, 1X/2X)

MEASUREMENTS
Finished Bust 36 (48, 56)"/91.5 (122, 142)cm
Finished Length 24 (27, 31)"/61 (68.5, 78.5)cm

MATERIALS
YARN
LION BRAND® Vanna's Choice®, 3½oz/100g balls, each approx 170yd/156m (acrylic)
- 7 (10, 14) balls in #133 Brick

NEEDLES
- One size 9 (5.5mm) circular knitting needle, 29"/73.5cm long, *or size to obtain gauge*
- One size 7 (4.5mm) circular knitting needle, 29"/73.5cm long

NOTIONS
- Stitch holders
- Tapestry needle

GAUGE
16 sts + 24 rows = 4"/10cm in Textured st using larger needle.
BE SURE TO CHECK YOUR GAUGE.

TEXTURED STITCH
(over an odd number of sts)
Row 1 (WS) K1, *p1, k1; rep from * to end.
Row 2 Knit.
Rep Rows 1 and 2 for Textured st.

K2, P2 RIB
(multiple of 4 sts plus 2)
Row 1 K2, *p2, k2; rep from * to end.
Row 2 K the knit sts and p the purl sts.
Rep Row 2 for K2, P2 Rib.

NOTES
1) Cardigan is worked in one piece beginning at lower edge of Back. Stitches are cast on for Sleeves then the piece is divided and the Fronts are worked separately down to lower edge.
2) A circular needle is used to accommodate the large number of stitches. Work back and forth on circular needle as if working on straight needles.

CARDIGAN
BACK
With larger needle, cast on 73 (97, 113) sts.
Row 1 (WS) Purl.
Row 2 Knit.
Beg with Row 1, work in Textured st until piece measures 16 (18, 21)"/40.5 (45.5, 53.5)cm from beg, end with a WS row.
Note As you continue working in Textured st, the st count will change. Thus, Row 1 won't always begin with a knit. Study how your work looks on both sides to determine which st to begin with.

Cast on for sleeves
Next Row (RS) Cast on 48 sts for Right Sleeve, k to end—121 (145, 161) sts.
Next Row Cast on 48 sts for Left Sleeve, k1, *p1, k1; rep from * to end of row—169 (193, 209) sts.
Beg with Row 2, work Textured st until piece measures 7 (8, 9)"/18 (20.5, 23)cm from cast-on sts for sleeves, end with a WS row.

Drapey Cardigan

Shape neck

Next Row (RS) K70 (80, 86) sts and sl those to a st holder for Right Shoulder, bind off center 29 (33, 37) sts, k to end of row for Left Shoulder—70 (80, 86) sts rem on needle for Left Shoulder.

Next Row Work even in Textured st across 70 (80, 86) sts for Left Shoulder.

Next Row Bind off 3 sts, k to end—67 (77, 83) sts.

Next Row Work even in Textured st.

Next Row Bind off 2 sts, k to end—65 (75, 81) sts.

Left Front

Work even in Textured st until sleeve measures 16 (18, 20)"/40.5 (45.5, 51)cm from cast-on sts for sleeve, end with a RS row.

BIND OFF LEFT SLEEVE

Next Row (WS) Bind off 48 sts for Left Sleeve, work Textured st to end—17 (27, 33) sts.

Work even in Textured st until Left Front measures 16 (18, 21)"/40.5 (45.5, 53.5)cm from bound-off sts for sleeve, end with a RS row.

Next row (WS) Purl.

Bind off.

Right Front

Sl 70 (80, 86) sts for Right Shoulder on larger needle, ready to work a WS row.

Next Row (WS) Bind off 3 sts, work Textured st to end—67 (77, 83) sts rem.

Next Row Knit.

Next Row Bind off 2 sts, work Textured st to end—65 (75, 81) sts.

Work even in Textured st until Right Sleeve measures same length as Left Sleeve, end with a WS row.

BIND OFF RIGHT SLEEVE

Next Row (RS) Bind off 48 sts, k to end—17 (27, 33) sts.

Work even in Textured st until Right Front measures same length as Left Front, end with a RS row.

Next Row Purl.

Bind off.

FINISHING

Cuffs

With smaller needle and RS facing, pick up and k 50 (58, 64) sts evenly across wrist edge of one sleeve.
Work in K2, P2 Rib for 6½"/16.5cm.
Bind off.
Rep for other sleeve.

Fold Cardigan across shoulder line. Sew side and sleeve seams, including cuffs.

Collar

With smaller needle and RS facing, pick up and k 134 (150, 174) sts evenly from lower edge of Right Front to center of back neck.

Work in K2, P2 Rib until collar measures 10 (11, 12)"/25.5 (28, 30.5)cm. Bind off.
From smaller needle and RS facing, pick up and k 134 (150, 174) sts evenly from center back neck lower edge of Left Front. Work as for first half of Collar.
Sew edges of collar tog at center of back neck.

Weave in ends. •

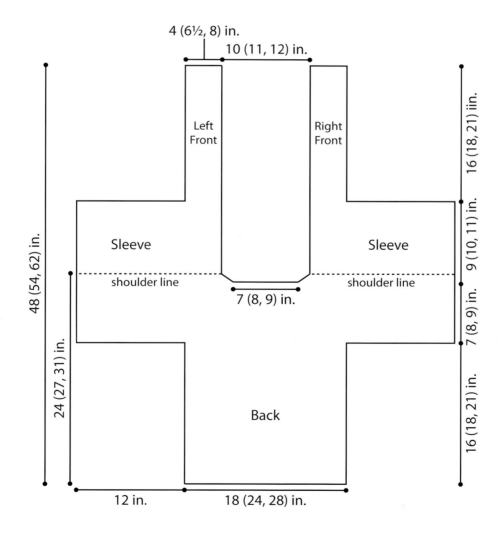

Back to Basics Knit Cardigan

Easy

SIZES
S/M (L/1X, 2X/3X, 4X/5X).

MEASUREMENTS
Finished Bust 40 (49, 56, 65)"/101.5 (124.5, 142, 165)cm
Finished Length (Back) 30"/76cm
Finished Length (Front) 28"/71cm

MATERIALS
YARN
LION BRAND® Wool-Ease® Thick & Quick®, 6oz/170g balls, each approx 106yd/97m (acrylic/wool)
• 6 (8, 8, 10) balls in #116 Succulent

NEEDLES
• One size 13 (9mm) circular knitting needle, 32"/81.5cm long, *or size to obtain gauge*
• One size 15 (10mm) circular knitting needle, 40"/101.5cm long

NOTIONS
• Stitch markers
• Tapestry needle

GAUGE
9 sts + 12 rows = approx 4"/10cm in St st with smaller needle.
BE SURE TO CHECK YOUR GAUGE.

K1, P1 RIB
(multiple of 2 sts plus 5)
Row 1 (WS) P2, k1, *p1, k1; rep from * to last 2 sts, p2.
Row 2 K2, p1, *k1, p1; rep from * to last 2 sts, k2.
Rep Rows 1 and 2 for K1, P1 Rib.

NOTES
1) The Back and two Fronts are worked first, then the shoulders are seamed. After seaming the shoulders, stitches for the Sleeves are picked up along the armhole edges.
2) The Back is 2"/5cm longer than the Fronts.
3) Circular needles are used to accommodate the large numbers of stitches. All pieces are worked back and forth in rows on a circular needle as if working with straight needles.
4) The front band is worked from stitches picked along the front and neck edges of the Cardigan.

CARDIGAN
BACK
With larger needle, cast on 45 (55, 63, 73) sts.
Work K1, P1 Rib until piece measures approx 5"/12.5cm from beg, end with a WS row as last row you work.
Change to smaller needle.
Work even in St st (k on RS, p on WS) until piece measures approx 28"/71cm from beg, end with a WS row as last row you work.

Shape back neck and shoulders
Row 1 (RS) K15 (19, 22, 26) sts for right shoulder, join 2nd ball of yarn and bind off center 15 (17, 19, 21) sts, k to end for left shoulder—15 (19, 22, 26) sts for each shoulder.
Note Work both shoulders AT THE SAME TIME with separate balls of yarn as following:
Row 2 Purl all sts of each shoulder.
Dec Row 3 (RS) On left shoulder, k to last 4 sts, ssk, k2; on left shoulder, k2, k2tog, k to end—14 (18, 21, 25) sts for each shoulder.
Rows 4 and 5 Rep Rows 2 and 3—13 (17, 20, 24) sts for each shoulder.

Back to Basics Knit Cardigan

Row 6 Purl all sts of each shoulder.
Bind off.

LEFT FRONT

With larger needle, cast on 21 (25, 29, 35) sts.
Work K1, P1 Rib until piece measures approx 3"/7.5cm from beg, end with a WS row as last row you work.
Change to smaller needle.
Work even in St st until piece measures approx 19½ (18¾, 18, 17½)"/49.5 (47.5, 45.5, 44.5)cm from beg, end with a WS row as last row you work.

Shape neck

Dec Row 1 (RS) K to last 4 sts, ssk, k2—20 (24, 28, 34) sts.

SIZES S/M (2X/3X) ONLY

Rows 2–4 Work even in St st.
Row 5 Rep Row 1—19 (27) sts.
Row 6 Purl.
Row 7 Rep Row 1—18 (26) sts.
Rows 8–19 Rep Rows 2–7 twice—14 (22) sts.
Rows 20–23 (20–27) Rep Rows 2–5 for 1 (2) more times—13 (20) sts.
Work even in St st until piece measures approx 28"/71cm from beg.
Bind off.

SIZE L/1X ONLY

Rows 2–4 Work even in St st.
Row 5 Rep Row 1—23 sts.
Rows 6–9 Rep Rows 2–5—22 sts.
Row 10 Purl.
Row 11 Rep Row 1—21 sts.
Rows 12–21 Rep Rows 2–11—18 sts.
Rows 22–25 Rep Rows 2–5—17 sts.
Work even in St st until piece measures approx 28"/71cm from beg.
Bind off.

SIZE 4X/5X ONLY

Row 2 Purl.
Row 3 Rep Row 1—33 sts.
Rows 4–6 Work in St st.
Row 7 Rep Row 1—32 sts.
Rows 8–31 Rep Rows 2–7 for 4 more times—24 sts.
Work even in St st until piece measures approx 28"/71cm from beg.
Bind off.

RIGHT FRONT

Make same as Left Front to shape neck.

Shape neck

Dec Row 1 (RS) K2, k2tog, k to end—20 (24, 28, 34) sts.
Complete Right Front same as Left Front, working neck dec at beg of dec rows.

SLEEVES

Sew shoulder seams.
Place markers on both side edges of Back and Fronts, 8"/20.5cm below shoulder seams.
Row 1 (RS) From RS with smaller needle, pick up and k 37 sts evenly along one armhole edge between markers.
Rows 2–4 Work even in St st for 3 rows.
Dec Row 5 (RS) K2, k2tog, k to last 4 sts, ssk, k2—35 sts.
Rep Rows 2–5 for 6 (6, 7, 6) more times—23 (23, 21, 23) sts.

Sizes S/M (L/1X) ONLY

Next 5 Rows Work even in St st.
Next Row Rep Row 5—21 sts.
Rep last 6 rows 1 (0) more time(s)—19 (21) sts.

All sizes

Work even in St st until Sleeve measures approx 15¼ (13¼, 12, 10)"/38.5 (33.5, 30.5, 25.5)cm.

Change to larger needle and work K1, P1 Rib for 3"/7.5cm.
Bind off.

FINISHING

Block piece to measurements.
Sew sleeve seams.
Sew side seams, leaving sides of lower ribbing open for side slits.

Front band

From RS with larger needle, beg at lower Right Front corner, pick up and k 58 (56, 54, 52) sts evenly Right Front edge to beg of V-neck shaping, (pick up and k 1, yo, pick up and k 1) all at beg of V-neck shaping for incr and pm in yo just made, pick up and k 25 (27, 29, 31) sts along right V-neck edge, pick up and k 19 (21, 23, 25) sts along back neck, pick up and k 25 (27, 29, 31) sts along left V-neck edge, (pick up and k 1, yo, pick up and k 1) all at beg of V-neck shaping for inc and pm in yo just made, pick up and k 58 (56, 54, 52) sts along Left Front edge to lower corner—191 (193, 195, 197) sts.

Rows 1–3 Beg with a WS row, work K1, P1 Rib.

Inc Row 4 (RS) *Work in K1, P1 Rib as established to first marker, (k1, yo, k1) in marked st; rep from * once more, work K1, P1 Rib as established to end of row—195 (197, 199, 201) sts.

Work even in K1, P1 Rib until band measures approx 2"/5cm.
Bind off.

Weave in ends. •

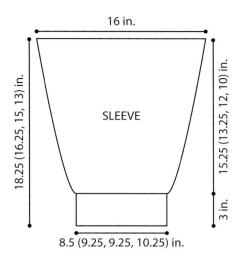

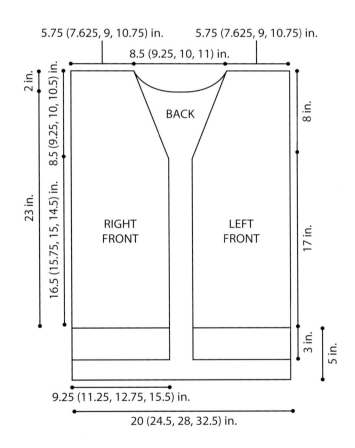

Freya Cardigan

Easy

SIZES
S (M/L, 1X/2X).

MEASUREMENTS
Finished Bust 48 (56, 62)"/122 (142, 157.5)cm
Finished Length 33 (34, 35)"/84 (86.5, 89)cm

MATERIALS
YARN
LION BRAND® Vanna's Choice®, 3½oz/100g balls, each approx 170yd/156m (acrylic)
- 6 (8, 9) balls in #405 Silver Heather (A)
- 3 (3, 4) balls in #404 Dark Grey Heather (B)

NEEDLES
- One size 6 (4mm) circular knitting needle, 36"/91.5cm long, *or size to obtain gauge*
- One size 4 (3.5mm) circular knitting needle, 36"/91.5cm long, *or size to obtain gauge*

NOTIONS
- Stitch holders
- Tapestry needle
- Waste yarn

GAUGES
- 16 sts + 24 rows = approx 4"/10cm in St st using larger needle.
- 19 sts = approx 4"/10cm in K2, P2 Rib using smaller needle.

BE SURE TO CHECK YOUR GAUGES.

LONG-TAIL PROVISIONAL CAST-ON
With a length of waste yarn, make a slip knot and place it on the right hand needle (in front of the last st made with the working yarn). Prepare to work a standard long-tail cast-on, placing the waste yarn over your thumb and the working yarn over your index finger. Cast on the number of sts indicated. The working yarn will make the loops for the new sts on the needle and the waste yarn will form a chain at the base of the new sts. Cut the waste yarn, leaving a long yarn tail.

K2, P2 RIB
(multiple of 4 sts)
Row 1 (RS) *K2, p2; rep from * to end.
Row 2 K the knit sts and p the purl sts.
Rep Row 2 for K2, P2 Rib.

NOTES
1) Cardigan is worked in 5 pieces: Back, 2 Fronts, and 2 Sleeves.
2) Each piece is worked back and forth in rows from the lower edge upwards.
3) The Back and Fronts are worked with yarn color A. The Sleeves are worked with yarn color B.
4) The pocket openings are worked directly onto each Front. The pocket lining is worked with yarn color B.
5) The front and neck band is worked from stitches picked up along the front and neck edges. The finished band is folded to the inside (WS) of the Cardigan and tacked in place.
6) Circular needles are used to accommodate the number of stitches. Work back and forth in rows on the circular needle just as if working on straight needles.

CARDIGAN
BACK
With smaller needle and A, cast on 92 (108, 120) sts. Work K2, P2 Rib until piece measures approx 3"/7.5cm from beg, end with a WS row as last row you work.

Change to larger needle.
Inc Row (RS) [K23 (27, 30), M1] 3 times, k to end—95 (111, 123) sts.
Work even in St st (k on RS, p on WS) until piece measures approx 22"/56cm from beg, end with a WS (purl) row as last row you work.

Shape armholes
Inc Row (RS) K1, M1, k to last st, M1, k1—97 (113, 125) sts.
Work even in St st for 5 rows.
Rep Inc Row—99 (115, 127) sts.
Rep last 6 rows for 3 (4, 5) more times—105 (123, 137) sts.
Continue in St st until armholes measure approx 7 (8, 9)"/ 18 (20.5, 23)cm, end with a WS row as last row you work.

Shape neck and shoulders
Continue in St st, and AT THE SAME TIME, bind off at beg of next row as follows:
2 (3, 3) sts 6 times.
3 (4, 4) sts 6 times.
4 (5, 6) sts 6 times.
6 (6, 8) sts 4 times.
12 (12, 12) sts 2 times.
Bind off rem 3 sts.

LEFT FRONT
With smaller needle and A, cast on 48 (56, 64) sts.
Work in K2, P2 Rib until piece measures approx 3"/7.5cm from beg, end with a WS row as the last row you work.
Change to larger needle.
Dec Row (RS) [K15 (17, 11), k2tog] 2 (2, 4) times, k to end—46 (54, 60) sts.
Work even in St st until piece measures approx 9"/23cm from beg, end with a WS row as last row you work.

Pocket opening
Row 1 (RS) K36 (40, 43), sl last 26 sts just knit onto holder, k to end of row.
Row 2 P10 (14, 17); using Long-Tail Provisional Cast-On, cast on 26 sts; p to end of row.
Work even in St st until piece measures same as Back to armholes, end with a WS row as last row you work.

Freya Cardigan

Shape armhole
Inc Row (RS) K1, M1, k to end—47 (55, 61) sts.
Work even in St st for 5 rows.
Rep Increase Row—48 (56, 62) sts.
Rep last 6 rows for 3 (4, 5) more times—51 (60, 67) sts.
Work even in St st until armhole measures same as Back armhole, end with a WS row as last row you work.

Shape neck and shoulder
Row 1 (RS) Bind off 2 (3, 3) sts, k to end—49 (57, 64) sts.
Row 2 and all WS rows Purl.
Rows 3–6 Rep Rows 1 and 2 twice—45 (51, 58) sts.
Row 7 Bind off 3 (4, 4) sts, k to end—42 (47, 54) sts.
Rows 9–12 Rep Rows 7 and 8 twice—36 (39, 46) sts.
Row 13 Bind off 4 (5, 6) sts, k to end—32 (34, 40) sts.
Rows 15–18 Rep Rows 13 and 14 twice—24 (24, 28) sts.
Row 19 Bind off 6 (6, 8) sts, k to end—18 (18, 20) sts.
Rows 21 and 22 Rep Rows 19 and 20.
Bind off rem 12 sts.

RIGHT FRONT
Work same as Left Front to shape armhole.

Shape armhole
Inc Row (RS) K to last st, M1, k1—47 (55, 61) sts.
Work even in St st for 5 rows.
Rep Inc Row—48 (56, 62) sts.
Rep last 6 rows for 3 (4, 5) more times—51 (60, 67) sts.
Work even in St st until armhole measures same as Back armhole, end with a RS row as last row you work.

Shape neck and shoulder
Row 1 (WS) Bind off 2 (3, 3) sts, p to end—49 (57, 64) sts.
Row 2 and all RS rows Knit.
Rows 3–6 Rep Rows 1 and 2 twice—45 (51, 58) sts.
Row 7 Bind off 3 (4, 4) sts, p to end—42 (47, 54) sts.
Rows 9–12 Rep Rows 7 and 8 twice—36 (39, 46) sts.
Row 13 Bind off 4 (5, 6) sts, p to end—32 (34, 40) sts.
Rows 15–18 Rep Rows 13 and 14 twice—24 (24, 28) sts.
Row 19 Bind off 6 (6, 8) sts, p to end—18 (18, 20) sts.
Rows 21 and 22 Rep Rows 19 and 20.
Bind off rem 12 sts.

SLEEVES
With smaller needle and B, cast on 32 (36, 40) sts.
Work in K2, P2 Rib until piece measures approx 3"/7.5cm from beg, end with a WS row as last row you work.
Change to larger needle.
Inc Row (RS) K1, M1, k to last st, M1, k1—34 (38, 42) sts.
Work even in St st for 3 rows.
Rep Inc Row—36 (40, 44) sts.
Rep last 4 rows for 2 (4, 6) more times—40 (48, 56) sts.
Work even in St st for 5 (5, 3) rows.
Rep Inc Row—42 (50, 58) sts.
Rep last 6 (6, 4) rows for 7 more times—56 (64, 72) sts.
Work even in St st until piece measures approx 15"/38cm from beg.
Bind off.

FINISHING
Pocket lining
From RS, return one set of pocket sts from holder to larger needle.

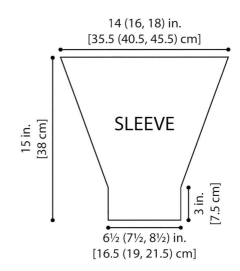

With B, work even in St st (so RS of pocket lining matches RS of Front) for approx 14"/35.5cm, end with a WS row as last row you work. Cut B, leaving a long tail for grafting. Carefully unravel waste yarn from pocket lining provisional cast-on and place sts onto other end of larger needle. Holding 2 needle tips parallel with WS of fabric held tog, thread a tapestry needle with long tail of B to graft using Kitchener stitch (see inside back cover)
Rep for second pocket.

Leaving 3 bound-off sts at center of Back unsewn, sew shoulder seams.

Front and neck band

From RS with smaller needle and A, beg at lower right front corner, pick up and k 127 (131, 135) sts evenly spaced along Right Front edge, pick up and k 2 sts across 3 bound-off sts of Back, then pick up and k 127 (131, 135) sts down Left Front edge—256 (264, 272) sts.

Rows 1–4 *K1, p1; rep from * across.
Change to B.
Row 5 Purl.
Row 6 *K1, p1; rep from * across.
Bind off.
Fold band to WS of Cardigan and tack in place.

Sew Sleeves into armholes.
Sew side and Sleeve seams.
Sew sides of pocket linings tog. Tack lower corners of each pocket lining to inside of Cardigan.

Weave in ends. •

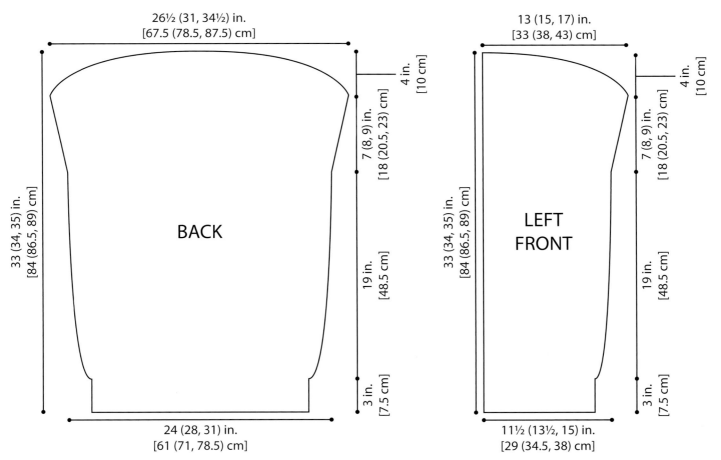

Light 'N Easy Cardigan

Easy

SIZES
S (M/L, 1X–3X).

MEASUREMENTS
Finished Bust 38 (46, 54)"/96.5 (117, 137)cm
Finished Length 18½ (20, 21)"/47 (51, 53.5)cm

MATERIALS
YARN
LION BRAND® Shawl in a Ball®, 5.3oz/150g balls, each approx 481yd/440m (cotton/acrylic/other)
• 2 (3, 4) balls in #300 Om Opal

NEEDLES
• One size 8 (5mm) circular knitting needle, 36"/91.5cm long, *or size to obtain gauge*
• One size 7 (4.5mm) circular knitting needle, 36"/91.5cm long

NOTIONS
• Stitch holders
• Tapestry needle

GAUGE
16 sts + 24 rows = approx 4"/10cm in rev St st using larger needle.
BE SURE TO CHECK YOUR GAUGE.

NOTES
1) Cardigan is worked in 2 Halves. The Halves are sewn together at center back to make the Cardigan.
2) Each Half is worked side to side from Sleeve to center back.
3) Halves are worked in reverse Stockinette stitch with garter stitch borders.
4) Circular needles are used to accommodate the large number of stitches. Work back and forth in rows on the circular needle as if working with straight needles.

CARDIGAN
LEFT HALF
Sleeve
With larger needle, cast on 42 (44, 46) sts.
Rows 1–10 Work in garter st (k every st every row).
Inc Row 11 (RS) P1, M1P, p to last st, M1P, p1—44 (46, 48) sts.
Rows 12–16 Beg with a WS (knit) row, work in rev St st (p on RS, k on WS).
Rows 17–88 (17–100, 17–112) Rep Rows 11–16 for 12 (14, 16) more times—68 (74, 80) sts.

Body
Row 1 (RS) Cast on 44 (46, 48) sts; beg over sts just cast on, k8, p to end—112 (120, 128) sts.
Row 2 Cast on 44 (46, 48) sts; beg over sts just cast on, k to end—156 (166, 176) sts.
Row 3 K8, p to last 8 sts, k8.
Row 4 Knit.
Rep Rows 3 and 4 until piece measures approx 6 (7½, 9)"/15 (19, 23)cm from cast-on sts of body, end with a RS row as last row you work.

Shape neck
Row 1 (WS) K78 (83, 88) sts and place these sts on a holder for Left Front edge sts, k to end—78 (83, 88) sts rem on needle.
Row 2 K8, p to end.
Dec Row 3 K1, ssk, k to end—77 (82, 87) sts.
Rows 4–9 Rep Rows 2 and 3 for 3 more times—74 (79, 84) sts.
Row 10 K8, p to end.

Light 'N Easy Cardigan

Row 11 Knit.
Rep Rows 10 and 11 until piece measures approx 9½ (11½, 13½)"/24 (29, 34.5)cm from cast-on sts of Body. Bind off.

RIGHT HALF
Work same as Left Half to Shape Neck, end with a WS row as last row you work.

Shape neck
Row 1 (RS) K8, p70 (75, 80) sts and place these last 78 (83, 88) sts on a holder for front opening, p to last 8 sts, k8—78 (83, 88) sts rem on needle.
Row 2 Knit.
Dec row 3 P1, p2tog, p to last 8 sts, k8—77 (82, 87) sts.
Rows 4–9 Rep Rows 2 and 3 for 3 more times—74 (79, 84) sts.
Row 10 Knit.
Row 11 P to last 8 sts, k8.
Rep Rows 10 and 11 until piece measures same length as Left Half.
Bind off.

FINISHING
Sew Halves tog at center back.

Front Band
From RS, with smaller needle, k78 (83, 88) Right Front edge sts from holder, pick up and k 25 (31, 37) sts evenly spaced along Back neck edge, k78 (83, 88) Left Front edge sts from holder—181 (197, 213) sts.
Work garter st for approx 3"/7.5cm.
With larger needle, bind off loosely.

Sew side and sleeve seams.
Weave in ends. •

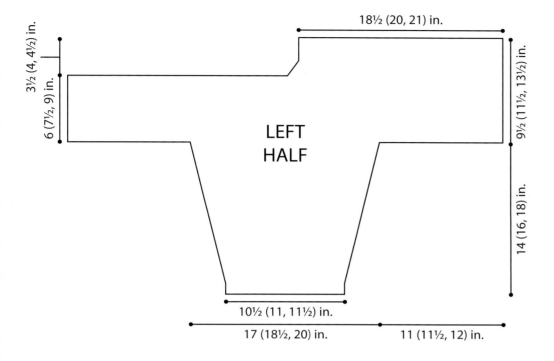
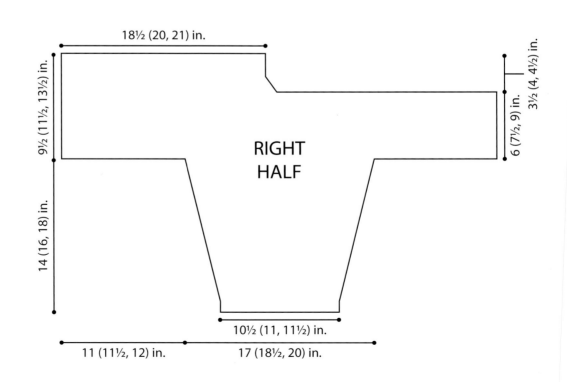

Lille Cardigan

Intermediate

SIZES
S (M/L, 1X/2X).

MEASUREMENTS
Finished Bust 39 (45, 51)"/99 (114.5, 129.5)cm
Finished Length 24 (25, 26)"/61 (63.5, 66)cm

MATERIALS
YARN
LION BRAND® Vanna's Choice®, 3½oz/100g balls, each approx 170yd/156m (acrylic)
- 6 (7, 9) balls in #300 Denim Mist

NEEDLES
- One pair size 9 (5.5mm) knitting needles, *or size to obtain gauge*

NOTIONS
- Stitch markers
- Tapestry needle

GAUGE
16 sts + 22 rows = approx 4"/10cm in St st.
BE SURE TO CHECK YOUR GAUGE.

STITCH GLOSSARY
1/3 plait (1 over 3 plait) Sl next st as if to knit, k3, lift slip st over 3 knit sts and off RH needle—1 st decreased.

EYELET PLAIT
(over a multiple of 4 sts)
Note You will be dec on Row 3 and inc on Row 4. Keep this in mind when counting sts.
Row 1 (RS) Knit.
Row 2 Purl.
Dec Row 3 *1/3 plait; rep from * to end
Inc Row 4 *P3, yo; rep from * to end.
Rep Rows 1–4 for Eyelet Plait.

NOTES
1) Cardigan is worked in 5 pieces: Back, 2 Fronts, and 2 Sleeves.
2) Front bands are worked in one with the Fronts.
3) Front bands are seamed to make the back neckband.
4) Edges of Cardigan are designed to roll softly to the WS.

CARDIGAN
BACK
Cast on 78 (90, 102) sts.
Knit 4 rows.
Beg with a RS (knit) row, work in St st (k on RS, p on WS) for 96 rows.

Shape armholes
Next Row (RS) Bind off 3 (5, 7) sts, k to end—75 (85, 95) sts.
Next Row Bind off 3 (5, 7) sts, p to end—72 (80, 88) sts.
Work even in St st until armholes measure approx 6 (7, 8)"/15 (18, 20.5)cm. Bind off.

LEFT FRONT
Cast on 46 (52, 58) sts.
Knit 4 rows.
Row 1 (RS) K to last 21 sts, pm, work Row 1 of Eyelet Plait to last st, k1.
Row 2 K1, work next row of Eyelet Plait to marker, sm, p to end.
Row 3 K to marker, sm, work next row of Eyelet Plait to last st, k1.
Rows 4–95 Rep Rows 2 and 3 for 46 more times.
Row 96 Rep Row 2.

Lille Cardigan

Shape armhole

Note When working armhole shaping your st count will depend on which row of the Eyelet Plait you are on. Remember that at the end of row 3 of Eyelet Plait pat, your st count will be slightly different than the st count given in our pattern since you will have decreased within the Eyelet Plait pattern.

Next Row (RS) Bind off 3 (5, 7) sts, k to marker, sm, work next row of Eyelet Plait to last st, k1—43 (47, 51) sts. Rep Rows 2 and 3 until armhole measures same as Back armhole, end with a Row 2 as last row you work.

Next Row (RS) Bind off 21 (25, 29) sts for shoulder, remove marker, work next row of Eyelet Plait to last st, k1—22 sts rem for neckband.

Next Row K1, work next row of Eyelet Plait to last st, k1. Rep last row until neckband measures approx 3¾"/9.5cm above bound-off sts of shoulder.
Bind off.

RIGHT FRONT

Cast on 46 (52, 58) sts.
Knit 4 rows.
Row 1 (RS) K1, work Row 1 of Eyelet Plait over next 20 sts, pm, k to end.
Row 2 P to marker, sm, work next row of Eyelet Plait to last st, k1.
Row 3 K1, work next row of Eyelet Plait to marker, sm, k to end.
Rows 4–97 Rep Rows 2 and 3 for 47 more times.

Shape armhole

Next Row (WS) Bind off 3 (5, 7) sts, p to marker, sm, work next row of Eyelet Plait to last st, k1—43 (47, 51) sts. Rep Row 3 once, then rep Rows 2 and 3 until armhole measures same as Back armhole, end with a RS row as last row you work.

Next Row (WS) Bind off 21 (25, 29) sts for shoulder (1 st rem on right needle), remove marker, work next row of Eyelet Plait to last st, k1—22 sts rem for neckband.

Next Row K1, work next row of Eyelet Plait to last st, k1. Rep last row until neckband measures same as Left Front neckband.
Bind off.

SLEEVES

Cast on 42 (46, 54) sts.
Knit 4 rows.
Beg with a RS (knit) row, work in St st for 6 rows.
Row 1 (RS) K15 (17, 21), pm, work Row 1 of Eyelet Plait over next 12 sts, pm, k15 (17, 21).
Row 2 P to marker, sm, work next row of Eyelet Plait to next marker, sm, p to end.
Row 3 K to marker, sm, work next row of Eyelet Plait to next marker, sm, k to end.
Rep Rows 2 and 3 until piece measures approx 3½"/9cm from beg, end with a Row 2 as last row you work.

Shape Sleeve

Inc Row (RS) K2, M1, k to marker, sm, work next row of Eyelet Plait to next marker, sm, k to last 2 sts, M1, k2—44 (48, 56) sts.

Next 11 (11, 9) Rows Rep Rows 2 and 3 for a total of 11 (11, 9) rows, end with a Row 2 as last row you work. Rep last 12 (12, 10) rows for 4 (5, 7) more times—52 (58, 70) sts.

Rep Row 3, then rep Rows 2 and 3 until piece measures approx 18 (18½, 19)"/45.5 (47, 48.5)cm from beg, end with a Row 2 as last row you work.

Shape Cap

Next Row (RS) Bind off 4 (4, 5) sts, k to marker, sm, work next row of Eyelet Plait to next marker, sm, k to end—48 (54, 65) sts.

Next Row Bind off 4 (4, 5) sts, p to marker, sm, work next row of Eyelet Plait to next marker, sm, p to end—44 (50, 60) sts.

Rep last 2 rows 2 (3, 3) more times—28 (26, 30) sts. Bind off.

FINISHING

Sew shoulder seams.

Matching center of Sleeve top to shoulder seam, sew in Sleeves.

Sew side and Sleeve seams.

Sew bound off ends of neckbands together. Sew lower edge of neckband to neck edge of Back.

Weave in ends. •

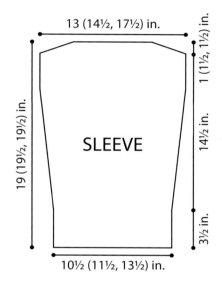

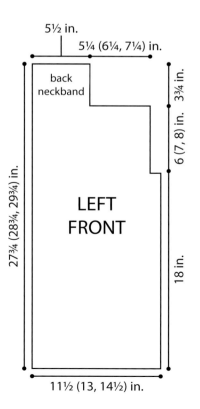

Reading Room Cardigan

Easy

SIZES
S/M (L/1X, 2X/3X).

MEASUREMENTS
Finished Bust 40 (48, 56)"/101.5 (122, 142)cm
Finished Length 29 (30, 31)"/73.5 (76, 78.5)cm

MATERIALS
YARN
LION BRAND® Wool-Ease® Thick & Quick® 6oz/170g balls, each approx 106yd/97m (acrylic/wool)
- 8 (10, 12) balls in #105 Glacier

NEEDLES
- One size 13 (9mm) circular knitting needle, 29"/73.5cm long, *or size to obtain gauges*

NOTIONS
- Stitch markers
- Stitch holders
- Tapestry needle
- 5 buttons, approx 1¼"/32mm diameter
- Sewing needle and thread

GAUGES
- 8 sts + 18 rows = approx 4"/10cm in garter st.
- 8 sts + 14 rows = approx 4"/10cm in St st.

BE SURE TO CHECK YOUR GAUGES.

NOTES
1) Cardigan is worked sideways in one piece, beginning at one Sleeve edge. The Sleeve is worked, then stitches are cast on for the Back and the Left Front. Work continues in one piece until the Left Front and Back are divided to shape the neck.

2) Stitches are cast on for the Right Front and this piece is worked separately, then joined to the Back. The join is made by simply working across the stitches of the Right Front, then continuing across the stitches of the Back (no sewing is involved in this join!). Work then continues in one piece across the Back/Right Front and the second Sleeve.

3) A circular needle is used to accommodate the width of the fabric. Work back and forth in rows on circular needle as if working with straight needles.

4) Cardigan is worked in garter stitch and Stockinette stitch. The gauge difference between gives a slight A-line shape to the Cardigan.

KNIT CAST-ON
*Insert right needle in next st on left needle; wrap yarn and pull through (as if knitting a st); transfer new st to left needle; rep from * for desired number of sts.

CARDIGAN
Cast on 22 (24, 26) sts.
Purl 1 row.

LEFT SLEEVE
Beg with a RS (knit) row, work in St st (k on RS, p on WS) for 16 rows.
Inc Row (RS) K1, kfb, k to last 2 sts, kfb, k1—24 (26, 28) sts.
Work in St st for 9 (7, 5) rows.
Rep Inc Row—26 (28, 30) sts.
Rep last 10 (8, 6) rows until you have 28 (32, 36) sts.
Work in St st for 6 rows.
Ridge Row (WS) Knit.
Work in St st for 2 rows.
Rep Inc Row—30 (34, 38) sts.
Ridge Row (WS) Knit.

Reading Room Cardigan

Work in St st for 3 rows.
Ridge Row (WS) Knit.
Rep last 4 rows once more.
Work in St st for 2 rows.
Rep Inc Row—32 (36, 40) sts.
Next Row (WS) Knit.

Cast-on for Back and Front
Using Knit Cast-On, cast on 42 sts for back—74 (78, 82) sts.
Row 1 (RS) Knit.
Using Knit Cast-on, cast on 42 sts for left front—116 (120, 124) sts.
Row 2 P34 (36, 38) for St st lower front of Cardigan, k24 for garter st (k every st every row) upper front of Cardigan, pm for center of shoulder, k24 for garter st upper back, p34 (36, 38) for St st lower back.
As you continue to work, slip the marker on each row as you come to it.
Row 3 Knit.
Row 4 P34 (36, 38), k48, p34 (36, 38).
Rep Rows 3 and 4 until garter st upper front section measures approx 7 (8½, 10)"/18 (21.5, 25.5)cm from cast-on sts, end with a WS row as last row you work.

Divide at Neck for Left Front and Back
Row 1 (RS) Work sts as established (in St st and garter st) to marker, then slip these 58 (60, 62) sts to a holder for Back, bind off 2 sts, work sts as established to end of row—56 (58, 60) sts rem on needle for Left Front.

LEFT FRONT
You will now be working over Left Front sts only.
Next Row (WS) Work sts as established (in St st and garter st) across.
Dec Row K2tog, work sts as established to end—55 (57, 59) sts.
Rep last 2 rows 2 more times—53 (55, 57) sts.
Work in established sts until upper Left Front garter st section measures approx 9¼ (11¼, 13¼)"/23.5 (28.5, 33.5)cm from cast-on edge.

Button band
Work in garter st for 7 rows.
Bind off.

BACK
Slip sts for back from holder onto needle and join yarn so that you are ready to work a WS row.
Dec Row (WS) K2tog, work sts as established to end—57 (59, 61) sts.
Work sts as established for 26 (30, 34) rows.
Inc Row (RS) Work in established patterns to last 2 sts, kfb, k1—58 (60, 62) sts.
Slip sts to a holder.

RIGHT FRONT
Cast on 53 (55, 57) sts.

Buttonhole band
Knit 3 rows.
Buttonhole Row (WS) K8, *k2tog, using Knit Cast-on, cast on 1 st, k6; rep from * 3 times, k2tog, using Knit Cast-on, cast on 1 st, k to end.
Knit 3 rows.

Next Row (WS) P34 (36, 38) for St st lower front, k to end for garter st upper front.
Work sts as established for 4 (6, 8) rows.
Inc Row (RS) K1, kfb, work as established to end—54 (56, 58) sts.
Next Row Work sts as established.
Rep last 2 rows 2 more times—56 (58, 60) sts.
Next Row (RS) Using Knit Cast-On, cast on 2 sts, work as established to end—58 (60, 62) sts.

JOIN RIGHT FRONT AND BACK
Next Row (WS) Work sts as established across Right Front, k24 Back sts from holder, p rem 34 (36, 38) Back sts from holder—116 (120, 124) sts.
Work sts as established until Right Front measures same as Left Front, end with a WS row as last row you work.

RIGHT SLEEVE

Next 2 Rows Bind off 42 sts, k to end—32 (36, 40) sts.

Dec Row (RS) K1, k2tog, k to last 3 sts, k2tog, k1—30 (34, 38) sts.

Work in St st for 2 rows.

Ridge Row (WS) Knit.

Work in St st for 3 rows.

Rep Ridge Row.

Rep last 4 rows once more.

Rep Dec Row—28 (32, 36) sts.

Work in St st for 2 rows.

Rep Ridge Row.

Work in St st for 6 rows.

Rep Dec Row—26 (30, 34) sts.

Work in St st for 9 (7, 5) rows.

Rep Dec Row—24 (28, 32) sts.

Rep last 10 (8, 6) rows 1 (2, 3) more times—22 (24, 26) sts rem.

Work in St st until Right Sleeve measures same as Left Sleeve.

Bind off.

FINISHING

Sew side seams.

With sewing needle and thread, sew buttons to Left Front button band opposite buttonholes.

Neck edging

From RS, pick up and k 36 (40, 44) sts spaced as evenly around neck edge. Without working any rows, bind off all sts as if to knit.

Weave in ends. •

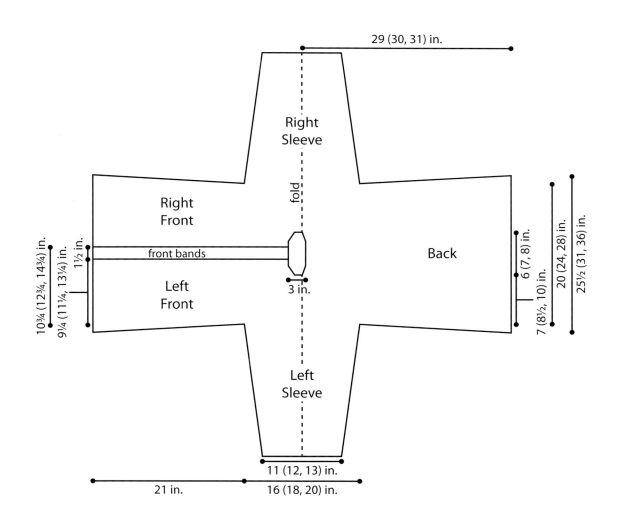

Vogar Cardigan

Easy

SIZES
S (M/L, 1X–3X).

MEASUREMENTS
Finished Bust 44 (52, 61)"/112 (132, 155)cm
Finished Length 21½ (22½, 23½)"/54.5 (57, 59.5)cm

MATERIALS
YARN
LION BRAND® Shawl in a Ball®, 5.3oz/150g balls, each approx 481yd/440m (cotton/acrylic/other)
• 2 (3, 3) balls in #307 Cleansing Quartz

NEEDLES
• One size 10 (6mm) circular knitting needle, 29"/73.5cm long, *or size to obtain gauge*

NOTIONS
• Stitch markers
• Stitch holders
• Tapestry needle
• 2 sew-on snaps, approx ⅝"/16mm diameter
• Sewing needle and thread

GAUGE
15 sts = approx 4½"/11.5cm and 17 rows = approx 4"/10cm in St st with 2 strands of yarn held tog.
BE SURE TO CHECK YOUR GAUGE.

K1, P1 RIB
(over an odd number of sts)
Row 1 (RS) K1, *p1, k1; rep from * to end.
Row 2 K the knit sts and p the purl sts.
Rep Row 2 for K1, P1 Rib.

GARTER RIDGE PATTERN
(over any number of sts)
Row 1 (WS) Knit.
Row 2 Knit.
Rows 3–5 Purl.
Row 6 Knit.
Row 7 (WS) Knit.

NOTES
1) Cardigan is worked in 5 pieces: Back, Left and Right Fronts, and 2 Sleeves.
2) All pieces are worked with 2 strands of yarn held together. For the 2 larger sizes, wind the 3rd ball of yarn into 2 equal size balls before beginning, or work with the beginning and ending strand of yarn from the 3rd ball.
3) A circular needle is used to accommodate the large number of stitches. Work back and forth in rows on the circular needle as if working on straight needles.

CARDIGAN
BACK
With 2 strands of yarn held tog, cast on 73 (87, 101) sts. Work K1, P1 Rib for 2 rows.
Beg with a RS (knit) row, work in St st (k on RS, p on WS) until piece measures approx 6½"/16.5cm from beg, end with a RS row as last row you work.
Work Rows 1–7 of Garter Ridge Pattern.
Work in St st until piece measures approx 13½"/34.5cm from beg, end with a WS row as last row you work.

Shape armholes
Inc Row 1 (RS) K1, M1, k to last st, M1, k1—75 (89, 103) sts.
Rows 2–8 Work even in St st for 7 rows.
Row 9 Rep Row 1—77 (91, 105) sts.
Rep Rows 2–9—79 (93, 107) sts.

Work even in St st until piece measures approx 19 (20, 21)"/48.5 (51, 53.5)cm from beg, end with a WS row as last row you work.

Shape shoulders
Row 1 (RS) Bind off 4 (5, 6) sts, k to end—75 (88, 101) sts.
Row 2 Bind off 4 (5, 6) sts, p to end—71 (83, 95) sts.
Rows 3 and 4 Rep Rows 1 and 2—63 (73, 83) sts.

Shape neck and shoulders
Place marker on each side of center 19 (21, 23) sts.
Row 1 (RS) Bind off 4 (5, 6) sts, k to first marker and place these 18 (21, 24) sts on a holder for right shoulder, bind off center sts between markers, k to end for left shoulder—22 (26, 30) sts rem on needle for left shoulder.

Left neck and shoulder
Row 1 (WS) Bind off 4 (5, 6) sts, p to end—18 (21, 24) sts.
Row 2 K1, ssk, k to end—17 (20, 23) sts.
Row 3 Bind off 5 (6, 7) sts, p to end—12 (14, 16) sts.
Rows 4 and 5 Rep Rows 2 and 3—6 (7, 8) sts.
Row 6 K1, ssk, k to end—5 (6, 7) sts.
Bind off rem 5 (6, 7) sts.

Right Neck and Shoulder
Return held right shoulder sts to needle. With WS facing, join 2 strands of yarn.
Row 1 (WS) P1, p2tog, p to end—17 (20, 23) sts.
Row 2 Bind off 5 (6, 7) sts, k to end—12 (14, 16) sts.
Rows 3 and 4 Rep Rows 1 and 2—6 (7, 8) sts.
Row 5 P1, p2tog, p to end—5 (6, 7) sts.
Bind off rem 5 (6, 7) sts.

LEFT FRONT
With 2 strands of yarn held tog, cast on 43 (51, 59) sts. Work K1, P1 Rib for 2 rows.
Row 1 (RS) K to last 6 sts, work K1, P1 Rib as established over last 6 sts for front band.
Row 2 Work K1, P1 Rib as established over first 6 sts, p to end.
Rep Rows 1 and 2, working in St st and keeping front band sts in K1, P1 Rib as established, until piece measures approx 6½"/16.5cm from beg, end with a RS row as last row you work.

Vogar Cardigan

Keeping front band sts in K1, P1 Rib as established, work Rows 1–7 of Garter Ridge Pattern.

Work in St st and keep front band sts in K1, P1 Rib as established, until piece measures approx 8"/20.5cm from beg, end with a WS row as last row you work.

Shape V-Neck

Dec Row 1 (RS) K to last 8 sts, k2tog, work K1, P1 Rib over last 6 sts—42 (50, 58) sts.

Rows 2–4 Keeping front band sts in K1, P1 Rib, work even in St st.

Row 5 Rep Row 1—41 (49, 57) sts.

Row 6 Keeping front band sts in K1, P1 Rib, p to end.

Row 7 Rep Row 1—40 (48, 56) sts.

Rows 8–19 Rep Rows 2–7 for 2 more times—36 (44, 52) sts.

Rows 20–24 Rep Rows 2–6—35 (43, 51) sts.

Shape armhole and neck

Row 1 (RS) K1, M1, k to last 8 sts, k2tog, work in K1, P1 Rib over last 6 sts

Rows 2–4 Keeping front band sts in K1, P1 Rib, work even in St st.

Dec Row 5 K to last 8 sts, k2tog, work K1, P1 Rib over last 6 sts—34 (42, 50) sts.

Rows 6, 8, 10, and 12 Keeping front band sts in K1, P1 Rib, p to end.

Row 7 Rep Row 5—33 (41, 49) sts.

Inc Row 9 K1, M1, k to last 6 sts, work K1, P1 Rib over last 6 sts—34 (42, 50) sts.

Row 11 Rep Row 5—33 (41, 49) sts.

Row 13 Rep Row 5—32 (40, 48) sts.

Rows 14–16 Keeping front band sts in K1, P1 Rib, work even in St st.

Row 17 Rep Row 1.

Row 18 Keeping front band sts in K1, P1 Rib, p to end.

Row 19 Rep Row 5—31 (39, 47) sts.

Rows 20–22 Keeping front band sts in K1, P1 Rib, work even in St st.

Row 23 Rep Row 5—30 (38, 46) sts.

Row 24 Keeping front band sts in K1, P1 Rib, p to end.

Size S ONLY

SHAPE SHOULDERS AND NECK

Row 1 (RS) Bind off 4 sts, k to last 8 sts, k2tog, work in K1, P1 Rib to end—25 sts.

Rows 2, 4, 6, and 8 Keeping front band sts in K1, P1 Rib, p to end.

Row 3 Bind off 4 sts, k to last 6 sts, work K1, P1 Rib—21 sts.

Row 5 Rep Row 1—16 sts.

Row 7 Bind off 5 sts, k to last 8 sts, k2tog, work K1, P1 Rib to end—10 sts.

Row 9 Bind off 5 sts, work in K1, P1 Rib to end—5 sts.

Row 10 Work K1, P1 Rib to end.

Bind off rem 5 sts.

Size M/L ONLY

Rep Rows 19–22—37 sts.

SHAPE SHOULDERS AND NECK

Row 1 (RS) Bind off 5 sts, k to last 8 sts, k2tog, work in K1, P1 Rib to end—31 sts.

Rows 2, 4, 6, and 8 Keeping front band sts in K1, P1 Rib, p to end.

Row 3 Rep Row 1—25 sts.

Row 5 Bind off 5 sts, k to last 6 sts, work K1, P1 Rib to end—20 sts.

Row 7 Bind off 6 sts, k to last 8 sts, k2tog, work K1, P1 Rib to end—13 sts.

Row 9 Bind off 6 sts, k2tog, work K1, P1 Rib to end—6 sts.

Row 10 Work K1, P1 Rib to end.

Bind off rem 6 sts.

Size 1X–3X ONLY

Rep Rows 19–24—44 sts.

Rep Rows 19 and 20—43 sts.

SHAPE SHOULDERS AND NECK

Row 1 (RS) Bind off 6 sts, k to last 6 sts, work in K1, P1 Rib to end—37 sts.

Rows 2, 4, 6, and 8 Keeping front band sts in K1, P1 Rib, p to end.
Row 3 Bind off 6 sts, k to last 8 sts, k2tog, work K1, P1 Rib to end—30 sts.
Row 5 Rep Row 3—23 sts.
Row 7 Bind off 7 sts, k to last 8 sts, k2tog, work K1, P1 Rib to end—15 sts.
Row 9 Bind off 7 sts, k2tog, work K1, P1 Rib to end—7 sts.
Row 10 Work K1, P1 Rib to end.
Bind off rem 7 sts.

RIGHT FRONT

With 2 strands of yarn held tog, cast on 43 (51, 59) sts.
Work K1, P1 Rib for 2 rows.
Row 1 (RS) Work K1, P1 Rib as established over first 6 sts for front band, k to end.
Row 2 P to last 6 sts, work K1, P1 Rib as established over last 6 sts.
Rep Rows 1 and 2, working in St st and keeping front band sts in K1, P1 Rib, until piece measures approx 6½"/16.5cm from beg, end with a RS row as last row you work.
Keeping front band sts in K1, P1 Rib as established, work Rows 1–7 of Garter Ridge Pattern.
Work in St st and keep front band sts in K1, P1 Rib as established, until piece measures approx 8"/20.5cm from beg, end with a WS row as last row you work.

Shape neck

Dec Row 1 (RS) Work K1, P1 Rib over first 6 sts, ssk, k to end—42 (50, 58) sts.
Rows 2–4 Keeping front band sts in K1, P1 Rib, work even in St st.
Row 5 Rep Row 1—41 (49, 57) sts.
Row 6 P to last 6 sts, work in K1, P1 Rib to end.
Row 7 Rep Row 1—40 (48, 56) sts.
Rows 8–19 Rep Rows 2–7 for 2 more times—36 (44, 52) sts.
Rows 20–24 Rep Rows 2–6—35 (43, 51) sts.

Shape Armhole and neck

Row 1 (RS) Work K1, P1 Rib over first 6 sts, ssk, k to last st, M1, k1.

Rows 2–4 Keeping front band sts in K1, P1 Rib, work even in St st.
Dec Row 5 Work K1, P1 Rib over first 6 sts, ssk, k to end—34 (42, 50) sts.
Rows 6, 8, 10, and 12 P to last 6 sts, work K1, P1 Rib to end.
Row 7 Rep Row 5—33 (41, 49) sts.
Inc Row 9 Work K1, P1 Rib over first 6 sts, k to last st, M1, k1—34 (42, 50) sts.
Row 11 Rep Row 5—33 (41, 49) sts.
Row 13 Rep Row 5—32 (40, 48) sts.
Rows 14–16 Keeping front band sts in K1, P1 Rib, work even in St st.
Row 17 Rep Row 1.

Vogar Cardigan

Row 18 P to last 6 sts, work K1, P1 Rib to end.
Row 19 Rep Row 5—31 (39, 47) sts.
Rows 20–22 Keeping front band sts in K1, P1 Rib, work even in St st.
Rep Row 5—30 (38, 46) sts.

Size S ONLY
SHAPE SHOULDERS AND NECK
Row 1 (WS) Bind off 4 sts, p to last 6 sts, work K1, P1 Rib to end—26 sts.
Dec Row 2 Work K1, P1 Rib over first 6 sts, ssk, k to end—25 sts.
Row 3 Rep Row 1—21 sts.
Row 4 P to last 6 sts, work K1, P1 Rib to end.
Row 5 Rep Row 1—17 sts.
Row 6 Rep Row 2—16 sts.
Row 7 Bind off 5 sts, p to last 6 sts, work K1, P1 Rib to end—11 sts.
Row 8 Rep Row 2—10 sts.
Row 9 Bind off 5 sts, work K1, P1 Rib to end—5 sts.
Row 10 Work K1, P1 Rib to end.
Bind off rem 5 sts.

Size M/L ONLY
Rep Rows 18–21—37 sts.

Shape Shoulders and Neck
Row 1 (WS) Bind off 5 sts, p to last 6 sts, work K1, P1 Rib to end—32 sts.
Row 2 Work K1, P1 Rib over first 6 sts, ssk, k to end—31 sts.
Row 3 Rep Row 1—26 sts.
Row 4 Rep Row 2—25 sts.
Row 5 Rep Row 1—20 sts.
Row 6 Keeping front band sts in K1, P1 Rib, work even in St st.
Row 7 Bind off 6 sts, p to last 6 sts, work K1, P1 Rib to end—14 sts.
Row 8 Rep Row 2—13 sts.
Row 9 Bind off 6 sts, work K1, P1 Rib to end—7 sts.
Row 10 Work K1, P1 Rib to last 2 sts, ssk—6 sts.
Bind off rem 6 sts.

Size 1X–3X ONLY
Rep Rows 18–23—44 sts.
Rep Rows 18 and 19—43 sts.

SHAPE SHOULDERS AND NECK
Row 1 (WS) Bind off 6 sts, p to last 6 sts, work K1, P1 Rib to end—37 sts.
Row 2 Keeping front band sts in K1, P1 Rib, work even in St st.
Row 3 Rep Row 1—31 sts.
Row 4 Work K1, P1 Rib over first 6 sts, ssk, k to end—30 sts.
Row 5 Rep Row 1—24 sts.
Row 6 Rep Row 4—23 sts
Row 7 Bind off 7 sts, p to last 6 sts, work K1, P1 Rib to end—16 sts.
Row 8 Rep Row 4—15 sts.
Row 9 Rep Row 7—8 sts.
Row 10 Work K1, P1 Rib to last 2 sts, ssk—7 sts.
Bind off rem 7 sts.

SLEEVES
With 2 strands of yarn held tog, cast on 35 (37, 39) sts.
Work K1, P1 Rib for 3 rows.
Inc Row (RS) K1, M1, k to last st, M1, k1—37 (39, 41) sts.
*Work even in St st for 3 (3, 1) row(s).
Rep Inc Row—39 (41, 43) sts.
Work even in St st for 3 (1, 1) row(s).
Rep Inc Row—41 (43, 45) sts.
Rep from * 2 (3, 4) more times—49 (55, 61) sts.
Work even in St st for 2 rows.

Garter ridge
Row 1 (WS) Knit.
Inc Row 2 K1, M1, k to last st, M1, k1—51 (57, 63) sts.
Rows 3–5 Purl.
Row 6 Rep Inc Row 2—53 (59, 65) sts.
Row 7 (WS) Knit.
Rows 8 and 9 Work even in St st.
Row 10 Rep Inc Row 2—55 (61, 67) sts.

Work even in St st until piece measures approx 10 (9½, 9)"/25.5 (24, 23)cm from beg, end with a WS row as last row you work.

Shape cap

Row 1 (RS) Bind off 9 (10, 11) sts, k to end—46 (51, 56) sts.
Row 2 Bind off 9 (10, 11) sts, p to end—37 (41, 45) sts.
Row 3 Bind off 6 (7, 8) sts, k to end—31 (34, 37) sts.
Row 4 Bind off 6 (7, 8) sts, p to end—25 (27, 29) sts.
Rows 5 and 6 Rep Rows 3 and 4—13 sts.
Bind off rem 13 sts.

FINISHING

Sew shoulder seams.

Place markers on Front and Back side edges approx 8 (9, 10)"/20.5 (23, 25.5)cm below shoulder seams. Sew tops of Sleeves between markers.

Sew side and Sleeve seams.

Weave in ends.

With sewing needle and thread, sew snaps to front bands. Sew one snap in lower ribbing and a 2nd to front band in line with center of Garter Ridge pattern. •

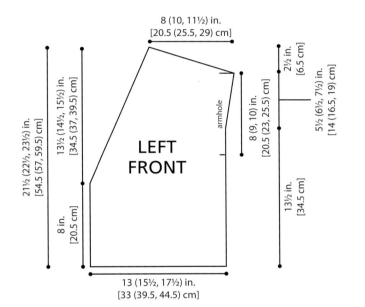

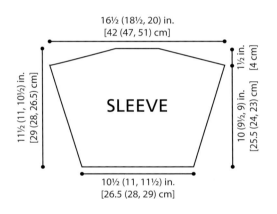

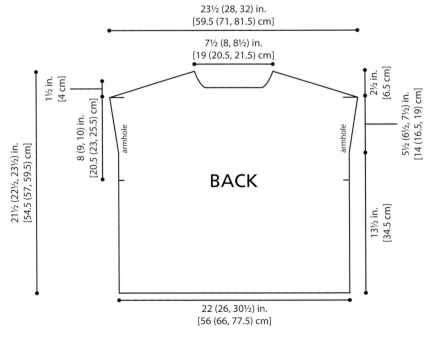

Top Down Raglan Cardigan

Easy

SIZES
S/M (L/1X).

MEASUREMENTS
Finished Bust 43½ (52)"/110.5 (137)cm
Finished Length (Back) 25½ (26½)"/65 (67.5)cm
Finished Length (Front) 22 (23)"/56 (58.5)cm

MATERIALS
YARN
LION BRAND® Wool-Ease® Thick & Quick®, 6oz/170g balls, each approx 106yd/97m (acrylic/wool)
- 7 (9) balls in #501 Sequoia

NEEDLES
- One size 13 (9mm) circular knitting needle, 36"/91.5cm long, *or size to obtain gauge*

NOTIONS
- Stitch markers
- Stitch holders
- Tapestry needle

GAUGE
9 sts + 12 rows = approx 4"/10cm in St st.
BE SURE TO CHECK YOUR GAUGE.

CABLE CAST-ON
*Insert right needle between first 2 sts on left needle, wrap yarn and pull through (as if knitting), transfer new st to left needle; rep from * for desired number of sts.

SEED RIB
(over an even number of sts)
Row 1 (RS) Knit.
Row 2 *K1, p1; rep from * to end.
Rep Rows 1 and 2 for Seed Rib.

SEED RIB
(over an odd number of sts)
Row 1 (RS) Knit.
Row 2 K1, *p1, k1; rep from * to end.
Rep Rows 1 and 2 for Seed Rib.

NOTES
1) Cardigan is worked in one piece from the top down.
2) Cardigan is worked to underarms then divided; Fronts, Sleeves, and Back are worked separately to lower edge.
3) Back of Cardigan is longer than front.
4) A circular needle is used to accommodate the large number of stitches. Work back and forth in rows on the circular needle just as if working on straight needles.

CARDIGAN
YOKE
Cast on 28 (33) sts.
Set-Up Row (WS) P2 (3) for Right Front, pm, p5 for Right Sleeve, pm, p14 (17) for Back, pm, p5 for Left Sleeve, pm, p2 (3) for Left Front.
Work in Seed Rib for 4 rows.
Inc row 1 (RS) *K to 1 st before next marker, kfb, sm, kfb; rep from * 3 more times, k to end—36 (41) sts.
Row 2 Purl.
Row 3 Rep Row 1—44 (49) sts.
Row 4 Rep Row 2.
Inc row 5 (RS) K1, M1, *k to 1 st before next marker, kfb, sm, kfb; rep from * 3 more times, k to last st, M1, k1—54 (59) sts.
Rows 6–25 (6–29) Rep Rows 2–5 for 5 (6) more times—144 (167) sts in Row 25 (29).
Row 26 (30) Rep Row 2.

Top Down Raglan Cardigan

LEFT FRONT

Row 1 (RS) K21 (25) for Left Front, place rem sts onto holder.

Row 2 Cast on 4 (5) sts onto left needle for underarm using Cable Cast-On, p to end—25 (30) sts.

Rows 3–10 Work in St st (k on RS, p on WS) for 8 rows.

Inc Row 11 (RS) K to last st, M1, k1—26 (31) sts.

Rows 12–20 Work in St st for 9 rows.

Row 21 Rep Row 11—27 (32) sts.

Work even in St st until Left Front measures approx 11½"/29cm from divide, end with a WS row as last row you work.

Work even in Seed Rib for 6 rows.

Bind off.

LEFT SLEEVE

Return next 31 (35) sts from holder to needle and join yarn so that you are ready to work a RS row.

Row 1 (RS) Cast on 4 (5) sts onto left needle for underarm using Cable Cast-On, k to end—35 (40) sts.

Row 2 Cast on 4 (5) sts onto left needle for underarm using Cable Cast-On, p to end—39 (45) sts.

Dec row 3 (RS) K1, k2tog, k to last 3 sts, ssk, k1—37 (43) sts.

Rows 4–10 Work in St st for 7 rows.

Row 11 Rep Row 3—35 (41) sts.

Rows 12–43 (12–51) Rep Rows 4–11 for 4 (5) more times—27 (31) sts.

Work even in St st until Sleeve measures approx 16 (17)"/40.5 (43)cm from divide, end with a WS row as last row you work.

Work even in Seed Rib for 6 rows.

Bind off.

BACK

Return next 40 (47) sts from holder to needle and join yarn so that you are ready to work a RS row.

Row 1 (RS) Cast on 4 (5) sts onto left needle for underarm using Cable Cast-On, k to end—44 (52) sts.

Row 2 Cast on 4 (5) sts onto left needle for underarm using Cable Cast-On, p to end—48 (57) sts.

Rows 3–10 Work in St st for 8 rows.

Inc row 11 (RS) K1, M1, to last st, M1, k1—50 (59) sts.

Rows 12–20 Work in St st for 9 rows.

Row 21 Rep Row 11—52 (61) sts.

Work even in St st until Back measures approx 13½"/34.5cm from divide, end with a WS row as last row you work.
Work even in Seed Rib for 10 rows.
Bind off.

RIGHT SLEEVE

Return next 31 (35) sts from holder to needle and join yarn so that you are ready to work a RS row.
Work same as for Left Sleeve.

RIGHT FRONT

Return next 21 (25) sts from holder to needle and join yarn so that you are ready to work a RS row.
Row 1 (RS) Cast on 4 (5) sts onto left needle for underarm using Cable Cast-On, k to end—25 (30) sts.
Rows 2–10 Work in St st for 9 rows.
Inc row 11 (RS) K1, M1, k to end—26 (31) sts.
Rows 12–20 Work in St st for 9 rows.
Row 21 Rep Row 11—27 (32) sts.

Work even in St st until Right Front measures approx 11½"/29cm from divide, end with a WS row as last row you work.
Work even in Seed Rib for 6 rows. Bind off.

FINISHING

Sew side and sleeve seams.
Sew underarm seams.

Front bands

Row 1 (RS) From RS, beg at lower Right Front corner, pick up and k 127 (138) sts evenly spaced along Right Front edge, around neck edge, and along Left Front edge to lower corner—127 (138) sts.
Beg with Row 2 (WS), work in Seed Rib for 5 rows. Bind off.

Weave in ends. •

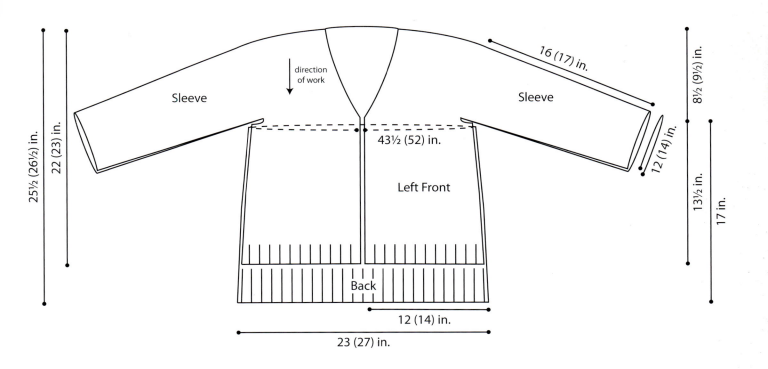

63

High Plains Cardigan

Easy

SIZES
S (M, L, 1X, 2X).

MEASUREMENTS
Finished Bust 36 (39, 44, 48, 52)"/91.5 (99, 112, 122, 132)cm
Finished Length 27 (28, 29, 30, 31)"/68.5 (71, 73.5, 76, 78.5)cm

MATERIALS
YARN
LION BRAND® Jeans®, 3½oz/100g balls, each approx 246yd/225m (acrylic) 【4】
- 2 (3, 3, 3, 4) balls each in #108 Brand New (A), #109 Stonewash (B), and #150 Vintage (C)
- 2 (2, 3, 3, 3) balls in #105 Faded (D)

NEEDLES
- One pair size 8 (5mm) knitting needles, *or size to obtain gauge*
- One pair size 6 (4mm) knitting needles

NOTIONS
- Stitch holders
- Tapestry needle

GAUGE
18 sts + 24 rows = approx 4"/10cm in Moss St using larger needles.
BE SURE TO CHECK YOUR GAUGE.

K1, P1 RIB
(over an even number of sts)
Row 1 (RS) *K1, p1; rep from * to end.
Row 2 K the knit sts and p the purl sts.
Rep Row 2 for K1, P1 Rib.

MOSS STITCH
(over an even number of sts)
Row 1 (RS) *K1, p1; rep from * to end.
Row 2 Rep Row 1.
Rows 3 and 4 *P1, k1; rep from * to end.
Rep Rows 1–4 for Moss St.

NOTES
1) Cardigan is worked in 5 main pieces: Back, 2 Fronts, and 2 Sleeves.
2) Pocket Linings are worked separately and joined to Cardigan as the Fronts are knit.

CARDIGAN
POCKET LININGS
With larger needles and A, cast on 22 (22, 26, 26, 26) sts. Work Moss St until piece measures approx 6 (6½, 7, 7½, 8)"/15 (16.5, 18, 19, 20.5)cm from beg, end with a Row 3 as last row you work.
Place sts on a st holder and cut yarn, leaving a long yarn tail.
Rep for 2nd pocket lining.

BACK
With smaller needles and A, cast on 90 (98, 108, 118, 126) sts.
Work K1, P1 Rib until piece measures approx 2"/5cm from beg, end with a WS row as last row you work.
Change to larger needles.
Beg with Row 1, work Moss St until piece measures approx 3 (3½, 4, 4½, 5)"/7.5 (9, 10, 11.5, 12.5)cm above ribbing, end with a WS row as last row you work.
Dec Row (RS) K1, k2tog, work Moss St as established to last 3 sts, ssk, k1—88 (96, 106, 116, 124) sts.

High Plains Cardigan

Work even in Moss St as established for approx 3"/7.5cm, end with a WS row as last row you work.

Note A-colored stripe will measure approx 6 (6 ½, 7, 7½, 8)"/15 (16.5, 18, 19, 20.5)cm from top of ribbing.

Change to B.
With B, rep Dec Row—86 (94, 104, 114, 122) sts.
With B, work even in Moss St as established until B-colored stripe measures approx 3"/7.5cm, end with a WS row as last row you work.
With B, rep Dec Row—84 (92, 102, 112, 120) sts.
With B, work even in Moss St until B-colored stripe measures approx 6"/15cm, end with a WS row as last row you work.

Change to C.
With C, rep Dec Row—82 (90, 100, 110, 118) sts.
With C, work even in Moss St as established until C-colored stripe measures approx 3"/7.5cm, end with a WS row as last row you work.
With C, rep Dec Row—80 (88, 98, 108, 116) sts.
With C, work even in Moss St as established until C-colored stripe measures approx 5"/12.5cm, end with a WS row as last row you work.

Shape Armholes

Row 1 (RS) Bind off first 4 (5, 6, 7, 8) sts, work Moss St to end—76 (83, 92, 101, 108) sts.
Row 2 Bind off first 4 (5, 6, 7, 8) sts, work Moss St to end—72 (78, 86, 94, 100) sts.
Rows 3 and 4 Bind off 2 sts, work Moss St to end—68 (74, 82, 90, 96) sts.
Rows 5–8 Bind off 1 st, work Moss St to end—64 (70, 78, 86, 92) sts.
Change to D.
With D, work even in Moss St until armholes measure approx 7 (7½, 8, 8 ½, 9)"/18 (19, 20.5, 21.5, 23)cm, end with a WS row as last row you work.

Shape Shoulders

Row 1 (RS) Bind off 6 (7, 8, 9, 10) sts, work in Moss St to end—58 (63, 70, 77, 82) sts.
Rows 2–6 Rep Row 1—28 (28, 30, 32, 32) sts.
Bind off.

LEFT FRONT

With smaller needles and A, cast on 50 (54, 58, 62, 66) sts. Work K1, P1 Rib until piece measures approx 2"/5cm from beg, end with a WS row as last row you work.
Change to larger needles.
Beg with Row 1, work Moss St until piece measures approx 6 (6½, 7, 7½, 8)"/15 (16.5, 18, 19, 20.5)cm from last ribbing row, end with a Row 2 of Moss st as the last row you work.

Attach pocket lining

Row 1 (RS) Work Moss St over first 14 (16, 16, 18, 20) sts, bind off center 22 (22, 26, 26, 26) sts, work Moss St to end.
Row 2 Work Moss St over first 14 (16, 16, 18, 20) sts, work Moss St as established over Pocket Lining sts on holder, work Moss st to end—50 (54, 58, 62, 66) sts.

Change to B.
With B, work even in Moss St until B-colored stripe measures approx 6"/15cm, end with a WS row as last row you work.

Change to C.
With C, work even in Moss St as established until C-colored stripe measures approx 5"/12.5cm, end with a WS row as tlast row you work.

Shape Armhole

Row 1 (RS) Bind off first 4 (5, 6, 7, 8) sts, work Moss St to end—46 (49, 52, 55, 58) sts.
Row 2 Work Moss St to end.
Row 3 Bind off 2 sts, work in Moss St to end—44 (47, 50, 53, 56) sts.
Row 4 Work Moss St to end.
Row 5 Bind off 1 st, work Moss St to end—43 (46, 49, 52, 55) sts.

Rows 6 and 7 Rep Rows 4 and 5—42 (45, 48, 51, 54) sts.
Row 8 Work Moss St to end.

Change to D.
With D, work even in Moss St until armhole measures approx 7 (7½, 8, 8½, 9)"/18 (19, 20.5, 21.5, 23)cm, end with a WS row as last row you work.

Shape shoulder

Row 1 (RS) Bind off 6 (7, 8, 9, 10) sts, work Moss St to end—36 (38, 40, 42, 44) sts.
Row 2 Work Moss St to end.
Rows 3–6 Rep Rows 1 and 2 twice—24 sts.

Collar extension

With D, work even in Moss St for approx 3 (3, 3½, 3½, 3½)"/7.5 (7.5, 9, 9, 9)cm, end with a WS row as last row you work.
Next Row (RS) Bind off 8 sts, work Moss St to end—16 sts.
Next Row Work Moss St to end.
Rep last 2 rows once more—8 sts.
Bind off.

RIGHT FRONT

Work same as Left Front to Shape Armhole, end with a RS row as last row you work.

Shape armhole

Row 1 (WS) Bind off first 4 (5, 6, 7, 8) sts, work Moss St to end—46 (49, 52, 55, 58) sts.
Row 2 Work Moss St to end.
Row 3 Bind off 2 sts, work Moss St to end—44 (47, 50, 53, 56) sts.
Row 4 Work in Moss St to end.
Row 5 Bind off 1 st, work Moss St to end—43 (46, 49, 52, 55) sts.
Rows 6 and 7 Rep Rows 4 and 5—42 (45, 48, 51, 54) sts.
Row 8 Work Moss St to end.
Change to D.
With D, work even in Moss St until armhole measures approx 7 (7½, 8, 8½, 9)"/18 (19, 20.5, 21.5, 23)cm, end with a RS row as last row you work.

Shape shoulder

Row 1 (WS) Bind off 6 (7, 8, 9, 10) sts, work Moss St to end—36 (38, 40, 42, 44) sts.
Row 2 Work in Moss St to end.
Rows 3–6 Rep Rows 1 and 2 twice—24 sts.

Collar extension

With D, work even in Moss St for approx 3 (3, 3½, 3½, 3½)"/7.5 (7.5, 9, 9, 9)cm, end with a RS row as last row you work.
Next Row (WS) Bind off 8 sts, work Moss St to end—16 sts.
Next Row Work Moss St to end.
Rep last 2 rows once more—8 sts.
Bind off.

SLEEVES

Note Throughout Sleeve, work in stripe sequence as follows: work 6"/15cm with A, then 6"/15cm with B, then 6"/15cm with C, and then rem with D.
With smaller needles and A, cast on 40 (44, 48, 52, 56) sts.
Work K1, P1 Rib until piece measures approx 2"/5cm from beg, end with a WS row as last row you work.
Change to larger needles.
Rows 1–5 Beg with Row 1, work Moss St for 5 rows.
Inc Row 6 (WS) K1, M1, work Moss St as established to last st, M1, k1—42 (46, 50, 54, 58) sts.
Continue in Moss St, following stripe sequence in note above AND AT THE SAME TIME, rep Inc Row every 6th row 11 more times—64 (68, 72, 76, 80) sts.
Work even in Moss St as established, changing color following stripe sequence in note above, until piece measures approx 17"/43cm from beg, end with a WS row as last row you work.

Shape cap

Rows 1 and 2 Bind off 4 (5, 6, 7, 8) sts, work Moss St to end—56 (58, 60, 62, 64) sts.
Rows 3 and 4 Bind off 2 sts, work Moss St to end—52 (54, 56, 58, 60) sts.
Rows 5–34 Bind off 1 st, work Moss St to end—22 (24, 26, 28, 30) sts.

High Plains Cardigan

Rows 35–38 Bind off 3 sts, work Moss St to end—10 (12, 14, 16, 18) sts.

Bind off.

FINISHING

Sew shoulder seams.

Sew ends of Collar Extensions tog, then sew lower edge of Collar Extensions to back neck edge.

Sew edges of Pocket Linings to WS of Fronts.

Sew in Sleeves. Sew side and Sleeve seams.

Weave in ends. •

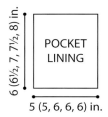

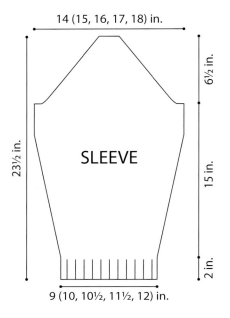

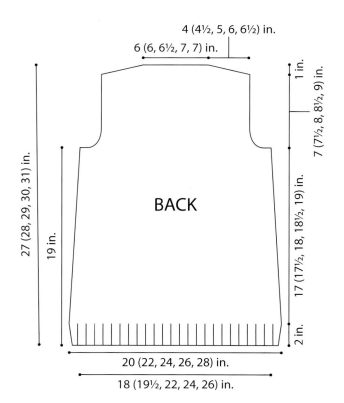

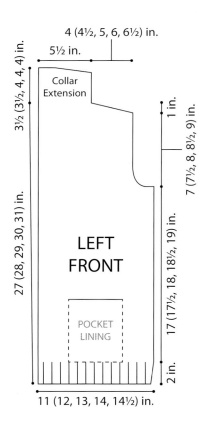